Literature Circles

Amy Seely Flint, Ph.D.

Teacher Created Materials, Inc.

Cover Design by Darlene Spivak

Made in U.S.A.

ISBN 1-57690-480-6

Order Number TCM 2480

www.teachercreated.com

Table of Contents

N p.6 −7
p8 use? for ob-instru.
p12 −21- exerpts

Introduction

Professional's Guide: Literature Circles addresses how to implement literature circles in the already overcrowded curriculum. Chapters highlight such issues as the classroom environment, the varying purposes for literature circles, patterns of talk, literature circles with emerging and independent readers, and alternative assessment. Throughout the chapters sample forms and examples are provided to illustrate some of the concepts.

Developing lifelong readers and writers is a primary goal in our classrooms. A literature circle is one possibility for fostering a love for literature and constructing meaningful insights into texts. Students are provided opportunities to explore and examine connections among texts and their own experiences. With the help of *Professional's Guide: Literature Circles,* I hope you discover the joy of discussing texts with your students.

Literacy Practices: New Approaches to Reading and Writing

Classrooms are busy places. Walking into an elementary school recently, I noticed in the hallways groups of students talking about books. As I entered a classroom transformed into a publishing center, students in all grades were working with volunteer editors from the community and local university. These students were sharing their drafts with the editors, talking about possible revisions, and scanning their own creations into the library system for future checkout. As I was making my way to the classroom I had come to visit, an upper-grade teacher stopped me to remind me that the Medieval Feast was coming up soon and her students were preparing their presentations. Finally, I arrived at my destination and encountered a class of primary students reading books with their upper-grade book buddies.

I sat down next to one of the pairs of students and quickly discovered that these two were not just reading the book—they were talking about the book.

I sat down next to one of the pairs of students and quickly discovered that these two were not just reading the book—they were talking about the book. The book being discussed was a new class favorite, *Chrysanthemum* (Henkes, 1996). The story is about a young mouse, Chrysanthemum, who discovers that her name is much more than a flower. Her name is a part of her identity and self-esteem.

These two students, one in kindergarten and one in fourth grade, were talking about their own names and how they encountered similar situations to Chrysanthemum's. Aurora, the fourth grader, mentioned that she never finds her name on nameplates and other items at different stores. The student in kindergarten, Emily, thought the friends in the story were mean and not really Chrysanthemum's friends. Aurora brought up the idea that it doesn't really matter what your name is, but if you are nice, people will like you. Both students constructed new understandings about the text and how they see themselves in the world. Personal connections were made to the story, and new insights emerged.

In leaving this classroom and the school, I am energized by what I observed. Students at this school are constructing meaning in interesting ways. Ideas are explored in a variety of forums, from literature discussions to personal writing to presentations. There is a sense of respect throughout the school; as a result, students are on task with their assignments and projects. The teachers do not appear to control the discussions or conversations, and in some cases, such as the groups in the hall, they are not present. As a result of these new structures and formats, students contribute to their own learning, bringing to the surface important ideas and interpretations that are meaningful to them.

Similar experiences are occurring throughout the country. This school, while forward thinking and progressive, is not an anomaly. There are many classrooms where teachers and students share responsibility for learning and teaching, where students are able to explore individual areas of interest, where teachers facilitate rather than dictate, and where the energy and enthusiasm for learning exceed expectations. You may teach in a school such as this, or you may know of classrooms and schools like the ones described. In either case, when students and teachers have opportunities for inquiry and reflection in reading and writing, understandings become tools for further exploration rather than ends unto themselves.

Readin' and Writin': It's Not How It Used to Be

No doubt you have heard the debates regarding the most effective ways to teach reading and writing. Many voices are in the debate, from educators and parents to journalists and politicians. At least once a week, there is an article or editorial in the local paper about how dismal the reading scores are for various groups of students. Publishers of educational books and textbooks have many titles addressing various approaches and methodologies for reading. Politicians are in the mix, trying to determine how to improve state test scores. The president issued a challenge to have all children

> There are many classrooms where teachers and students share responsibility for learning and teaching, where students are able to explore individual areas of interest, where teachers facilitate rather than dictate, and where the energy and enthusiasm for learning exceed expectations.

reading by the end of third grade reading. Best practices and theories are subjects of debate among those in the universities' research communities. Teachers and administrators wonder what they should be doing in the classrooms. Parents are concerned because of what they read and hear in the media. At the center of all this are young readers and writers.

Questions fuel the debate. What is the best approach to reading and literacy development? Is there a "one size fits all" method to reading? What about those who are readers but rarely choose to read? What about those students who seem to struggle with the entire process? These questions are but a sampling of what is asked on a regular basis. While the direction of this book is to offer ideas and strategies for literature circles, it is important to reflect on our theoretical positions and how these positions impact the way we think about literacy and literature discussions in the elementary grades.

Regardless of which side of the debate you find yourself agreeing with, it is clear we have dramatically changed the way we think about and teach reading and writing in our classrooms.

Those of us who have been teaching for awhile may recognize the circularity of educational ideas and theories. It seems that there are no new ideas in the field but only old ones revisited and reviewed with new eyes and new intentions. Dating back to the early part of the twentieth century, Dewey (1916) and other pioneers (Thorndike, 1921; Gray, 1924; Gates, 1937) suggested that reading and learning are complex, multifaceted processes. Dewey talked of the importance of authentic experiences in learning. Gray explored the relationship between theory and practice as related to phonics and reading materials, while Gates discussed testing and assessment. The range of ideas examined by the pioneers in the field provided contemporaries with opportunities to refine their thinking and build on current needs and practices.

Contemporaries, like our forefathers, also focus on a broad range of issues, from the role of language acquisition and reading to studies on comprehension, readability of text, and motivation and engagement (Hymes, 1972; Halliday, 1975; Pearson, 1985; Guthrie, Ng, McCann, Van Meter, & Alao, 1995). The last decade or so has centered on best practices and what constitutes effective reading programs. Some argue for more "skills," including phonemic awareness and phonics. Others suggest that there is more to the reading process than decoding and that it is critical to consider the role of background experience and prior knowledge when constructing meaning. Regardless of which side of the debate you find yourself agreeing with, it is clear we have dramatically changed the way we think about and teach reading and writing in our classrooms.

Reading and writing used to be taught only through direct instruction. Teachers often placed students in ability groups. Students individually completed work sheets that addressed comprehension and vocabulary. Reading involved knowledge of discrete skills with little connection to other texts or outside experiences. A prescribed reading program, generally a basal series, was used to teach reading.

Now we see teachers using authentic literature selections as part of the reading curriculum. Students are grouped not according to reading ability but according to interest. They are reading multiple texts on common themes, discovering similarities and differences. Bringing in prior experiences and background knowledge is an important aspect of the process and is welcomed during literature discussions. Students understand texts in complex and multiple ways.

> **It is through our interactions with others that new understandings about the world emerge.**

Writing was approached in a similar way. Grammar, spelling, and punctuation were stressed and viewed as the critical aspect of effective writing. Students practiced writing by completing grammar exercises in textbooks. Writing was often a task that did not hold much relevance or meaning. The audience for the document was usually the teacher, and there were limited opportunities for sharing rough drafts or celebrating authorship. As with reading, we have reconceptualized our approaches to writing. Writer's Workshop (Graves, 1983; Calkins, 1994) and Authoring Cycle (Short, Harste, & Burke, 1996) have enabled teachers and learners to view writing as a process. Students are using life experiences to write about and publish. There are opportunities for collaboration and revision with peers and teachers through conferences. The conferences focus on various aspects from design and structure of the document to content and mechanics. Additionally, students come to realize that writing is a purposeful endeavor.

Social Constructivism: The Impetus for New Directions

Why the changes? One significant difference is a transforming belief system in how children learn. Vygotsky (1978), a leading theorist in child development and learning, talked about the role of social interaction as a critical aspect of learning. In this work, Vygotsky suggested that learning is a social endeavor. It is through our interactions with others that new understandings about the world emerge. He introduced "zone of proximal development" as the distance between what a child can do alone and what a child can do with guidance by an adult or more capable peer. Shared reading events in kindergarten exemplify this idea. Young learners are able to "read" the story with a teacher, but if left alone, they might not engage in such actions or behaviors. You might recognize this as "scaffolding" (Bruner, 1986). Scaffolding is not only between adults and children but can also occur among children. For example, a multi-age grouping of students creates opportunities for more advanced readers to scaffold ideas for the less capable ones, further emphasizing the notion that learning is a social endeavor.

As part of the socially situated environment, language is the primary tool for thinking. Children grapple with and perceive new experiences as they communicate and share with others. Students engage in language-mediated activities, including speaking, reading, writing, and listening. They use these to relate events to their own experiences, their own worlds (Britton, 1993). When children have opportunities to talk and negotiate ideas, new understandings are constructed. To illustrate, a group of fourth graders read a chapter of *Mouse and the Motorcycle* (Cleary, 1965). They begin talking about how the different editions of the book have different pictures. An earlier edition of the story has the mouse without a helmet; a later one shows the mouse wearing a bike helmet. A conversation ensues about why the mouse is now wearing a helmet, and the students conclude that a long time ago, people did not have to wear helmets and so the author did not make the mouse wear one either. Students appropriate each other's ideas and understandings to discuss the benefits of wearing helmets when riding their own bikes. They use their experiences and language to construct negotiated interpretations of the text. New interpretations emerge.

These culturally determined practices impact and shape how we engage in discussions in the classroom.

In addition to rethinking the role of language and social interaction in learning and literacy development, our classrooms have different faces. We now have more students who speak a primary language other than English and who have different experiences and backgrounds. Bruner (1986) talks about how language not only defines our experiences but also defines our culture. Our patterns of language use are tied to and reinforced by our culture, community, and cultural patterns. How we orally retell stories, conceptualize space and time, and engage in problem solving depends on our cultural beliefs and practices (Heath, 1983). These culturally determined practices impact and shape how we engage in discussions in the classroom. Students who tell stories in structures which are alternative to the linear, time-sequenced structure may experience frustration because their approaches may not be recognized as story structures. Some cultures believe it is not acceptable to talk in the classroom setting without being formally recognized by an adult or teacher. So students participating in discussions without teacher presence may not respond to comments in the conversation. Varying ways of interacting and communicating influence how literature discussions are enacted in the classroom.

Reader Response

Reading and writing are interpretive acts. When we see the word "read," how do we know how to pronounce it? If it is in the sentence *I read the chapter last night,* we say it as /red/. If we see the word in the sentence *I will read the chapter tonight*, we pronounce the word /rēd/. The way we say a word is determined by the context, the surrounding words in the sentence. Our knowledge of language tells us that when the event occurred in the past, we use a different pronunciation than when the event is to occur in the future. As expert readers we are scanning passages of text to determine if the word is /red/ or /rēd/.

Let's expand this idea to think about whole texts. Reading stanzas of poems sometimes leaves us bewildered. Many of us can recall experiences of reading passages and constructing interpretations only to discover the teacher had a different interpretation in mind. Was there a secret to understanding the poem? Why did we have different interpretations for the same words?

Writing is also an interpretive act. The writer determines how ideas and concepts are presented in written text. What we want others to experience through our writing shapes how and what we write. If I want someone to know my emotional state, I might boldface the text to emphasize the emotion. As the writer, I can help the reader interpret the text a particular way, but I can not be guaranteed that he or she will read it that way.

> **Responding to text is an active process of thinking, talking, and writing, all of which contribute to constructing interpretations that are shared and negotiated in socially situated environments, namely the classroom.**

Theories of reader response help explain the varied interpretations we hold as readers and writers (Rosenblatt, 1978, 1994; Fish, 1980; Langer, 1995; Many, 1989). Responding to text is an active process of thinking, talking, and writing, all of which contribute to constructing interpretations that are shared and negotiated in socially situated environments, namely the classroom. Students respond to texts based on their own prior experiences, background knowledge, and purposes for the reading event. Rosenblatt (1978) suggests that when someone is engaged in the reading event, he or she brings not only his or her own experiences about the world but also entertains a multitude of possible interpretations offered by the text. The meaning, then, is not "in" the text or "in" the reader but happens as a result of a transaction between the reader and the text. Within the transaction, a change occurs in the reader's understandings as text and experiences come together.

Judith Langer (1995) extends these ideas to think about reader response as a process of envisionment. She defines envisionment as "text worlds in the mind and they differ from individual to individual.... Envisionments are dynamic sets of related ideas, images, questions, disagreements, anticipations, arguments, and hunches that fill the mind during every reading, writing, speaking, or other experience when one gains, expresses, and shares thoughts and understandings" (p. 9).

Within envisionment-building classrooms, students and teachers engage in discussions with opportunities to reconsider and interpret text from multiple perspectives. As students and teachers read a text such as *Island of the Blue Dolphins* (O'Dell, 1960), they bring to the discussion individual understandings and knowledge about Native Americans, survival, friendships, and determination. Teachers may want students to recognize their own abilities in difficult situations; students may focus on the friendship between Karana, the main character, and the wild dogs. Through discussion students and teachers come to value divergent interpretations.

Literature Circles: The Whats and Whys

Literature discussions, literature circles, book talks, etc., are essentially the same concept. In this book, the terms literature discussions and literature circles will be used interchangeably. Essentially, a literature circle is a forum in which students have opportunities to discuss and share interpretations and understandings of text. Similar to other innovations and strategies in the classroom, literature circles vary in intent and structure, depending on the teacher and classroom environment. In some classrooms, literature discussion time is reminiscent of traditional three-group reading structures. The teacher determines the text to be read, asks the questions, and accepts only those responses that are aligned with his or her thinking. "Round robin" reading may also be incorporated into this time

In other classrooms, students select the text to read and conduct their own discussions. They choose their group members based on interest in the text rather than on reading ability. Students determine how much to read for the discussion and talk about what they found interesting or problematic. There is not a pre-determined agenda for the discussion, so the conversation brings up many different aspects of the text.

Literature discussions vary in design and implementation because of the teacher's goals and purposes for the event. The composition and number of students in a group, the genre of text discussed, the direction of the discussion, whether writing is a part of the event, and the opportunities for students to disagree, challenge, defend, and inquire are choices and decisions made by the teacher. With all the different ways of thinking about and implementing literature circles, it is possible to see a multitude of strategies and activities under the same overarching term or definition.

> Essentially, a literature circle is a forum in which students have opportunities to discuss and share interpretations and understandings of text.

Lapp, Flood, Ranck-Buhr, Van Dyke, and Spacek (1997) outline three important reasons why literature discussions are significant and meaningful to effective reading programs. First, they suggest that literature discussions and book clubs strengthen students' understandings of text. Reflecting on a study by Samway et al., (1991) students commented that opportunities to talk about the text were critical to helping them become knowledgeable and lifelong readers. Second, literature discussions increase students' oral language development and use. Students engage in conversations rich with complex language and ideas. These discussions encourage students to explore a range of semantic and syntactic devices in language structure. Third, participating in book clubs and discussions supports Vygotsky's (1978) social learning theory. "The way we talk and interact with others becomes internalized and helps shape the way we think and learn" (Lapp et al., 1997).

"The way we talk and interact with others becomes internalized and helps shape the way we think and learn" (Lapp et al., 1997).

Questions to Consider

Many of you may already implement one of these forms of literature discussions or literature circles into your curriculum. How would you describe your literature circles, book talks, story reading events? Please take a minute to answer the following questions about what occurs in your classroom.

- Describe your classroom environment.
- What materials do you use in your reading program?
- How do you group your students for reading?
- Who determines what text or story will be read during "reading time?"
- What goals do you have for your students as they participate in these discussions?
- When you talk about a chapter or a book with a group of students, who asks the majority of the questions?
- When you think about questions that are asked, how many are at the factual and literal level? How many are interpretive and applicative?
- How do you structure literature discussions in your classroom? What do you do before, during, and after the discussion?
- What opportunities do your students have to make connections among texts and outside experiences?
- What opportunities do students have to incorporate writing and art into their literature discussions?
- In what ways do you assess students as they participate in discussions and literature circles?

How did you answer these questions? For some of you, the remaining chapters will be a review and a chance to reflect on what you already have established in the classroom. Others of you might discover new ways of thinking about literature discussions and story reading events. At the very least, the focus of this book is to offer some ideas and strategies for implementing and maintaining literature discussions as a viable and significant aspect of your literacy program.

The Remaining Chapters

As mentioned, the purpose of the book is to provide you with new ways of thinking about literature discussions, reading and writing programs, and to suggest possible strategies for making the discussions successful endeavors. Chapter two addresses classroom organization and purposes teachers establish for literature circles. In essence the chapter lays the groundwork for implementing effective literature discussions in the classroom. Chapter three talks about the patterns of talk and discourse in classroom environments. There is a considerable amount of research in this area, and in this chapter we explore different ways to increase students' participation in literacy events.

The next two chapters, four and five, provide strategies and ideas for implementing literature discussions and circles in your classroom. Chapter four describes literature circles with emerging readers and writers in primary classrooms. Students in these grades are enthusiastic and excited about participating in literacy events. Many are beginning to explore the conventions of text. Interactive story reading events provide an accessible way into the text. The chapter offers strategies to involve young students in the story as well as to encourage them to explore alternative sign systems such as art and drama.

Chapter five, then, discusses how to implement effective and meaningful literature discussions with independent readers. There are many ways to organize the discussions and activities for these students. Possibilities for narrative- and expository-based discussions will be shared in the context of theme cycles and text sets. It is important to recognize that many of these students are successful readers but are choosing not to engage in reading events. These students are often known as the reluctant readers—those that can read but very often choose not to read.

It would be incomplete if we did not discuss issues of assessment. Assessment is a critical aspect of anything you do in the classroom. Chapter six, therefore, talks about how to assess students as they engage in literature discussions. Strategies for documenting the

> As mentioned, the purpose of the book is to provide you with new ways of thinking about literature discussions, reading and writing programs, and to suggest possible strategies for making the discussions successful endeavors.

content of the discussion as well as how students participate will be shared. These strategies become the evidence that is necessary for assessment and evaluation of students' growth in literacy and language arts.

Finally, the last chapter brings together the ideas and activities for implementing effective and meaningful literature discussions. We revisit our purposes for establishing literature circles and how these purposes ultimately drive the direction of the discussion. We reflect on how to incorporate literature circles and discussions in all grades, kindergarten through six, and we review assessment practices. Concluding the book will be ideas for further consideration.

Concluding Remarks

The challenge is offered. How can we establish effective literature discussions in our classrooms where our students are in charge of their learning and meaning is constructed? Can our classrooms be places where students can explore and examine text in multiple ways with multiple results? This first chapter has opened up the possibilities.

Students, teachers, the classroom community, and the text all come together as meanings are constructed and negotiated.

Reflecting on Vygotsky's (1978) understandings of "zone of proximal development" and the social nature of learning, we can see that literature discussions provide the setting for bringing together individual interpretations to construct negotiated understandings. Ideas presented on reader response suggest that our learners construct their own understandings of text and the world around them based on prior experiences, knowledge, and cultural values. Students, teachers, the classroom community, and the text all come together as meanings are constructed and negotiated.

You were asked to think about your own classrooms and the kinds of discussions you currently implement. I hope you accept the challenge and continue exploring the many possibilities for effective and meaningful literature discussions.

We're Ready to Begin

Congratulations. The challenge is accepted. You are interested in reflecting on your own understandings of literature discussions and circles. The questions and your responses in chapter one will provide the general topics for this chapter and remaining chapters. Classroom environments, group composition, materials selected for the conversations, issues of choice, and what your underlying goals and purposes are for the literature discussions are the focus of this chapter.

- Describe your classroom environment.
- How do you group your students for reading?
- What materials do you use in your reading program?
- Who determines what text or story will be read during "reading time?"
- What goals do you have for your students as they participate in these discussions?

Literature Circle Environments

In the school I described in the first chapter, students and teachers are enthused and excited to learn. Even the discussions in the hallways

Classroom environments, group composition, materials selected for the conversations, issues of choice, and what your underlying goals and purposes are for the literature discussions are the focus of this chapter.

provide excitement for the learners. The students and teachers in this school actualize their beliefs about learning and teaching by establishing structures that enable them to engage in meaningful literacy events.

start vi

Risktaking, trust, and community are critical aspects of successful literature discussion environment. When a discussion is meaningful, risks are involved. A student may say something that appears to have little relevance, if any, to the ongoing discussion. Yet the student making the comment is confident that he or she has contributed to the negotiated understanding of the text. Other students may consider the interpretation to be viable and want to push the thinking further to better understand the possible connection. For those involved, taking and accepting risks moves the discussion towards more complex insights and interpretations.

Along with risktaking and trust is a belief that students are more likely to engage in discussions and literacy events when they view themselves as members of a community.

Teachers who are innovative in their thinking about students and curriculum are often risktakers. They realize that not every idea or activity is successful, but they are willing to explore, experiment, and persevere. For example, a group of fourth graders inexperienced with literature discussions were unsure of how to move beyond "my favorite part." It took almost a month of perseverance and patience before students began talking about character motivation, the author's intentions, and underlying themes.

There is also an underlying belief system of trust. When students are free to talk about anything that is interesting, problematic, or important to them, they begin to discover that discussions can be more than recalling details from the story. You can trust students to bring into the discussion points of view that will invite others to act and respond. Believing that students have insights that are meaningful is a critical aspect of the literature discussion environment.

Along with risktaking and trust is a belief that students are more likely to engage in discussions and literacy events when they view themselves as members of a community. Vygotsky (1978) explained that learning and literacy development occur more effectively in socially situated environments. Establishing community in the classroom facilitates interactions among students and teachers. One possibility to promote community is "community share" (Raphael and Goatley, 1997) whereby students and teachers as a whole class develop, share, and refine interpretations emerging from various literature discussions. Students learn community norms, how to participate in the community, and construct concepts of themselves and their peers as literate members (McMahon, 1997). Students are able to connect with others, and ideas as issues are raised and challenged. Opportunities to participate in events such as "community share" provide a public and social forum to explore ideas, develop shared understandings, and assume multiple ways of interacting.

Who's in the Group? And What Are We Reading?

In most cases literature circles and discussions are group endeavors. As in traditional reading groups, students work together while reading a particular story. Group composition and the types of texts read influence the outcomes of discussions—whether they are meaningful literacy events or not.

stop

Grouping Structures

Grouping students for effective instruction can be a whole other book by itself. Teacher Created Materials has a Professional's Guide on cooperative learning (Grisham and Molinelli, 1995) that offers different strategies and configurations for students working in cooperative groups. Cooperative learning effectively helps students value and respect each other as well as themselves. In terms of literature discussions and circles, we want to consider not only who is in the group but also if the whole class is discussing one text or if students are reading and discussing different texts as part of the reading curriculum.

Responses and language skills are often less diverse in ability groups, thereby limiting the possibility to hear multiple interpretations.

Researchers and teachers have raised questions in the past decade or so about the rigidity of ability groups (Hiebert, 1983; Atwell, 1987; Morrice and Simmons, 1991). When students are grouped according to perceptions of reading ability, issues of empowerment, amount of instruction, and type of instruction surface. There are also different expectations for the groups. Students in a low reading group are generally provided with more decontextualized skills-based instruction than students in a higher reading group. Additionally, Vygotsky's (1978) notion of students learning from "more capable peers" is not realized when students of the same abilities are grouped together. Responses and language skills are often less diverse in ability groups, thereby limiting the possibility to hear multiple interpretations.

Conversely, heterogeneous groupings for literature discussions provide opportunities for students to share and interact with those not so similar to themselves. Expanding the group to include students who excel in different areas, such as academic, social, and language, enables students to explore multiple responses and contribute to the richness of the discussion. Riordan-Karlsson (1997) discovered that students develop points of access with each other. In other words, students have criteria they use to determine if peers are viable partners for activities. Some of the criteria include perceptions of

13

each other's academic performance, behavior, and friendship circles. In the student selection of partners and other group members, it becomes critical for teachers to consider these criteria when establishing literature circles.

A strategy for composing heterogeneous groups is to create a grid rating students' abilities in academic, social, and language adeptness. It is desirable to have students representing a range of skills and abilities. Imagine a class reading *Charlotte's Web* (White, 1952). Tonya, Carlos, Rodney, Deshon, Maria, and Lawrence are potentially a group.

Name	Academic	Social	Language
Tonya	H	M	H
Carlos	L	H	M
Rodney	H	L	H
Deshon	L	H	H
Maria	M	L	L
Lawrence	M	L	L

H = high ability; expert; competent; well liked

M = average ability; able to work with most students

L = low ability; not competent in skills; not able to work well with peers

Tonya and Rodney provide a foundation for understanding the text, while Carlos and Deshon keep the conversation flowing. Maria and Lawrence understand the text fairly well and benefit from participating in group conversations to improve their own language and social skills. Students who are stronger academically are challenged to explain ideas to peers who struggle with the subtleties of the story, such as the many levels of friendship. Those requiring support in language are able to hear the target language in academic settings. As these students work together, they complement and push each other's thinking.

Not all literature discussions are whole class affairs. Oftentimes there are multiple texts and discussions going on in the classroom. The groupings are not so much decided by the teacher but rather by students' interests. Students select the story they are interested in reading and form groups based on those interests.

To illustrate this, imagine a second grade class interested in studying ecology. The teacher identifies three appropriate texts based on the theme. Students decide which of the three they are interested in reading and talking about. One group might be reading *Where Once There Was a Wood* (Fleming, 1996), another group reading *The Great Kapok Tree* (Cherry, 1990), and a third group reading *A River Ran Wild* (Cherry, 1991). Students come together to discuss issues raised in the texts. Those reading *Where Once There Was a Wood* might bring up issues of overbuilding and damage to the natural environment. Similar ideas might be expressed in the discussion group reading *A River Ran Wild,* while those reading *The Great Kapok Tree* might discuss issues of endangered habitats. When students select texts based on interests, the grouping becomes flexible. Students have opportunities to work with different peers throughout the instructional year.

Reading Materials

Children's literature (often referred to as "trade books") is the material for literature circles and story time in classroom settings. The majority of literature discussions involve texts written in a narrative structure—ones that tell a story. Many of us have made the shift in our reading programs from published basal textbooks to trade books but are left wondering which selections will be most effective for the discussions. Texts for literature circles should be of high quality and recognized as such. When assembling your narrative collection, you should ensure that the collection contains books of genuine literary merit, is likely to be meet the interests of your students, and represents events and characters of diverse ethnicity, cultural heritage, class, and gender (Wells, 1997).

Cullinan and Galda (1994) describe how children's literature should be a mirror and a window. As a mirror the story can reflect events and emotions experienced by those reading the story. When sixth graders read *Ice* (Naylor, 1995), discussions can emerge about families, growing up, and communication. Many students will be able to relate to Chrissa's feelings of inadequacy and anger when her father leaves the family and her mother does not know how to talk with her about his desertion.

Texts can also be windows on the world. Through literature we come to explore and learn about events and the world that we may not experience in real life. We can experience the lives of others whose cultures and histories differ from our own. While first graders are listening to *The Butterfly Seeds* (Watson, 1995), they can imagine what it must be like to leave their homes, country, and family members to start a new life. For some this story may not be a window

Through literature we come to explore and learn about events and the world that we may not experience in real life.

but a mirror. In any case, children's literature provides opportunities to read about the big issues facing us, "including but not limited to, love, hate, greed, justice, generosity, friendship, revenge, growing up, dying, and facing challenges" (Raphael & Boyd, 1997, p. 74).

In addition to narrative texts for literature discussions, expository texts are also important sources. Children are naturally curious about their world around them, and expository texts can help explain some of the social and hard science phenomena that occur. Seymour Simon's *Sharks* (1995) reveals that sharks are not the deadly monsters we think but, instead, fascinating creatures. In our reading programs, however, we tend not to utilize expository texts as often as we should because we find our students struggle to comprehend the material. There are a variety of reasons why expository text appears to be more difficult for our students to comprehend, including text patterns, difficult terminology, and lack of personal connection (Raphael & Hiebert, 1996). Including expository texts for discussions is one possibility for alleviating some of the problems associated with using them in the classroom. *Stop*

> **Children are naturally curious about their world around them, and expository texts can help explain some of the social and hard science phenomena that occur.**

Identifying texts that are of high quality in literary and/or expository elements can be accomplished through a variety of sources. *Children's Books: Awards and Prizes* (Children's Book Council, 1992) lists approximately 125 award winning books, mostly at the intermediate level. *The Reading Teacher* (published by International Reading Association) and *Language Arts* (published by National Council of Teachers of English) are two sources that provide monthly columns about exceptional new books on the market. *The Reading Teacher* also publishes "Children's Choices" (October issue) and "Teachers' Choices" (November issue), awards given annually to recent "favorites" among children and teachers. Below is a sample of children's favorites published in 1996.

Beginning Readers (ages 5–6)

DeCesare, Angelo   *Anthony the Perfect Monster* (Random House)

Grossman, Bill   *My Little Sister Ate One Hare* (Crown)

Young Readers (ages 6–8)

Henkes, Kevin   *Lilly's Purple Plastic Purse* (Greenwillow)

Novak, Matt   *Newt* (HarperCollins)

Wood, Audrey   *Bright and Early Thursday Evening: A Tangled Tale* (Harcourt Brace)

Intermediate Readers (ages 8–10)

Armstrong, Robb   *Drew and the Bub Daddy Showdown* (HarperCollins)

| Heckman, Philip | *Waking Upside Down* (Atheneum) |
| Lorbiecki, Marybeth | *Just One Flick of a Finger* (Dial) |

<u>Advanced Readers (ages 10–13)</u>

| Pipe, Jim | *In the Footsteps of the Werewolf* (Copper Beach/Millbrook) |
| Spinelli, Jerry | *Crash* (Knopf) |

Other awards for excellent literature and illustrations include the Newbery Award, which honors books for literary excellence; the Caldecott Medal, awarded to the illustrator of the most distinguished picture book; and the Coretta Scott King Illustrator Award is given to an illustrator of African descent. Colleagues and librarians are also good resources for identifying and selecting quality literature for your reading program and literature discussions.

start

Giving Students Choice

Choice is a critical aspect of engagement. Students are much more likely to engage in an activity if they have some decision-making power within the activity. Making decisions and choices provides them with a sense of empowerment, and empowerment leads to engagement. Opportunities to make decisions regarding their own learning encourage students to be thoughtful and reflective learners. When students have some choices about what they are going to read for literature discussions, their level of engagement in the texts may increase.

> Making decisions and choices provides them with a sense of empowerment, and empowerment leads to engagement.

When I talk about choice, I am not suggesting abdicating responsibility for the curriculum. There is a fine balance between letting students decide their curriculum and the direction it will follow and meeting national, state, and district standards. Most first and second graders are enamored by dinosaurs. How can that interest be incorporated into the standards outlined in national, state, and district documents? To effectively meet the needs of your students as well as addressing the standards, you may want to consider your curriculum in a holistic framework. As you plan your long-range goals, you might identify some places that students can decide what the themes and texts will be. Maybe you want students to select every other theme, or maybe you want to only have them select texts for the theme. Or perhaps you want to determine the theme and the texts but have students decide which of the texts they want to read. All of these options assume that your curriculum is organized by theme cycles whereby particular concepts are explored through a variety of texts and activities.

Reflecting on your curriculum as a whole enables you to identify those aspects of the theme or text that are aligned with various standards. No single text or one theme has to address each standard. The holistic approach reduces some of the tension; if you know your students are going to have opportunities to explore important concepts when they read *Number the Stars* (Lowry, 1989) or *Daniel's Story* (Matas, 1993), you can let them select from the Goosebumps series by R. L. Stine. While these texts do not hold the literary merit we want students to be familiar with, it is important to provide some places where they feel empowered and have a sense of ownership. Students may even begin to identify those literary aspects for themselves. When fourth graders discussed *Mouse and the Motorcycle* (Cleary, 1965) and then selected *Night of Terror Tower* (Stine, 1995), they realized that the characters in the Goosebumps story were flat and difficult to talk about. Students gained ownership of their learning by coming to their own conclusions about the literary merits of the stories.

What we want our students to gain from the experience will depend on what we determine are the salient aspects of the discussion.

Establishing Purposes for Literature Circles

The move to incorporate authentic literature selections into our literacy program has many benefits. Wells (1997) identifies three such benefits. First, students discover and examine worlds beyond their individual experiences. They have opportunities to imagine other possibilities. Second, literature provides us with a way to understand our own cultural heritage and histories. We can read stories that help to shape who we are and what we are becoming. Third, reading authentic literature increases our aesthetic appreciation because these are works of art with the authors and illustrators crafting new artifacts. We can find our own voices as writers by reading and discussing others' texts.

These benefits, however, come with costs. As we incorporate more literature into our curriculum, we need to be cognizant of our own purposes and goals for the literature discussions and circles. When we utilize published reading programs, the purposes are laid out for us. Within the teacher's manual, the goals of the program as well as the outcomes are clearly stated. Using trade books as the main source of material for our literacy program requires us to establish the purposes and directions for the texts and discussions.

The purposes we have for our literature discussions are broadly defined. What we want our students to gain from the experience will depend on what we determine are the salient aspects of the discussions. Teachers and learners adopt a viewpoint or way of perceiving information and knowledge. This viewpoint is known as stance. They define their own reasons and purposes for engaging in the literacy event. There are many different kinds of stance, ranging from personal to contextual in any given reading and writing event, but for purposes of this professional's guide, the focus will be on personal and instructional stances.

As part of her work on reader response, Louise Rosenblatt (1978) suggests personal stance is a reflection of the reader's purpose for engaging in the reading event. What we pay attention to within the text can be placed on a continuum from efferent to aesthetic. The continuum offers a range of ways of responding to and engaging with text. An efferent stance is defined as reading to gain information. An illustration of this stance is reading a science textbook passage on photosynthesis. When we read this passage, we are reading to gain specific information about the process. On the other end of the continuum is an aesthetic stance. Reading a story for its escapist qualities is reading with an aesthetic stance. We focus our attention on the images, feelings, emotions, and ideas that are not explicitly foregrounded in the text but provide the reader with a sense of "living through" the story. Reading a favorite story to our students is reading with an aesthetic stance. We want them to enjoy the story and language the text provides. You can maintain flexibility when adopting a personal stance. While we initially position ourselves on the continuum as adopting a predominately efferent or predominately aesthetic stance, we often shift as we read, write, and discuss texts.

The instructional stance you adopt directly influences the students' purpose and attention towards the story and discussion.

As you think about your own discussions and circles, what are the salient aspects of the literature you want your students to reflect upon? What do you want your students to come away with? These questions help to shape your instructional stance. The objectives you envision for a particular literacy event depend on the instructional stance you adopt (Ruddell & Ruddell, 1995). Your instructional stance is aligned with your personal stance. You may want your students to focus on the content and to remember information presented in the story. In this case, a predominately efferent instructional stance is adopted. Or you may want to encourage your students to identify with character motivations and events, and so you adopt a predominately aesthetic instructional stance. The instructional stance you adopt directly influences the students' purpose and attention towards the story and discussion.

Understanding this issue of stance is critical to how our literature circles are shaped and formed. How many of us have wanted our students to enjoy literature, to immerse themselves in the beautiful language of the text, to recognize the powerful effects of literature on their own lives? I am fairly confident that this is a goal and a desire for most of us. We ourselves are literature lovers. We want our students to be, as well. In our planning and implementing of theme cycles and literature discussions, the viewpoints and purposes we have for texts seem to get pushed into the background and sometimes forgotten.

One incident I am reminded of occurred in a third grade class where they were reading *Charlotte's Web* (White, 1952). The teacher and students engaged in literature discussions and journal writing for most of the chapters. As part of the journal writing, the students were to provide a summary of the chapter, difficult vocabulary words, and a personal reaction. The discussions often focused on the responses in these journals. One young reader, Jillian, began reading *Charlotte's Web* with a predominately aesthetic stance. She sympathized with Wilbur in the chapter when it rained and wondered how Charlotte knew how to spell the words. At the end of the theme unit, Jillian wrote in her journal, "Hooray Charlotte is dead. The book is over. Hooray."

The stances you adopt and, subsequently, the ones your students adopt emerge through the types of questions asked during literature discussions or in writing activities.

What happened to Jillian is not uncommon. The teacher emphasized the summaries rather than the personal reactions. For Jillian it became important to write a "good" summary rather than to talk about her own reactions and impressions of the story. The predominately efferent stance was more salient in the discussions, and the aesthetic stance slipped into the background. Towards the end of the story Jillian and her peers became disengaged from the story, and constructing meaningful interpretations was lost.

The stances you adopt and, subsequently, the ones your students adopt emerge through the types of questions asked during literature discussions or in writing activities. Questions focused on the details of the story (What kind of animal is Templeton? What did Charlotte write the first time? What does runt mean?) encourage students to assume an efferent stance towards the text. The intention of the discussion is to identify particular aspects of the story and to recall them with accuracy. Providing opportunities for students to adopt an aesthetic stance towards the text can be promoted through more interpretive questions (Why do you think Wilbur was upset that Charlotte could not attend the fair? How does Wilbur respond to Charlotte's request to care for her babies? Is this something you would do if you were Wilbur?). Responses to these questions require students to imagine and experience the "lived through" aspect of the text.

Concluding Remarks

Establishing literature discussions and circles in our classrooms is more than merely reading a story and asking/responding to questions. It is critical to the effectiveness and meaningfulness of the discussions that we compose groups of varying abilities, including academic, social, and language skills. These heterogeneous groups provide all students with opportunities to participate in the discussions. Creating grids or charts to rate our students is an approach that helps us determine balanced groups.

Involving students in the decision-making process is also important to maintaining literature circles throughout the instructional year. They can select their own texts to read or determine which group to work with. Considering your curriculum in a holistic manner helps ensure that you are meeting the demands of state and national standards while at the same time providing space in the curriculum for student choice.

Most important, however, is the stance and purpose you establish for the literature discussions. Rosenblatt's (1978) continuum provides us with a way of thinking about the nature of our questions and responses, whether they are predominately efferent or predominately aesthetic. Research shows that when our students adopt predominately aesthetic stances towards literature, they have higher levels of understanding and higher levels of engagement (Cox & Many, 1989b, 1992). There are times when we want to gather information and times when we want to read for enjoyment. What we want our students to gain from the experience and the types of questions we ask significantly influences the success of these discussions.

What we want our students to gain from the experience and the types of questions we ask significantly influences the success of these discussions.

21

"We Can Say *Anything*": Patterns of Classroom Talk

Literacy events are shaped not only by the content to be learned or discussed but also by the level of participation and engagement within the event.

Students and teachers participate in a multitude of literacy events within the classroom setting, including literature discussions and circles. Literacy events are shaped not only by the content to be learned or discussed but also by the level of participation and engagement within the event. Students are often restricted in what they can talk about and in the direction of the conversation. In this chapter, various patterns of talk among teachers and students and different structures for discussions will be offered.

- When you talk about a chapter or a book with a group of students, who asks the majority of the questions?
- When you think about the questions that are asked, how many are at the factual and literal level? How many are interpretive and applicative?

Talking in the Classroom—I-R-E

Vygotsky (1978) argued for the role of language in developing meaning and higher order thinking. It is through language that we come to understand concepts and our place in the world. Our social interaction with others shapes and defines meanings of words and how they are used in various contexts. Language, we know, is central to learning—used for some purpose and in some situation.

Students' participation in classroom events plays a significant role in how meanings are constructed and negotiated in the socially situated context of the classroom. Students discover how to gain access into the discussion, how to take turns talking so that ideas are heard, and how to share relevant ideas and information with the group. Those of us who have taught the pre-school and kindergarten aged children recognize that these actions and behaviors are very often learned in our classrooms.

There is quite a bit of research on how students and teachers participate in classroom talk and the effects of such participation (Mehan, 1979; Cazden, 1988; Almasi, 1996; Raphael, Brock, & Wallace, 1997). One pattern prevalent in many classrooms, particularly during discussions and reading events, is what Mehan (1979) and Cazden (1988) termed the I-R-E structure. I-R-E stands for *initiate, respond*, and *evaluate*. A teacher generally takes the lead in a discussion and *initiates* a question. A student is asked to *respond* to the question, and then the teacher *evaluates* whether the response was appropriate or satisfactory. This pattern of talk is often seen in classrooms where a transmission model of teaching is in place, where the teacher is perceived as owning the information and the students are empty vessels to be filled.

One pattern prevalent in many classrooms, particularly during discussions and reading events, is what Mehan (1979) and Cazden (1988) termed the I-R-E structure.

The following interchange occurred in a fourth grade classroom with a small group of students and the teacher. The focus of the discussion was to talk about events occurring in a chapter from *Otherwise Known as Sheila, the Great* (Blume, 1972). Notice the I-R-E structure.

Mrs. Kingston (teacher): What's going on in that chapter? What's happening Robert? What's happening in the chapter?

Robert: She is learning to put her face in the water and blow out bubbles.

Mrs. Kingston: Learning to put her face in the water and blow out bubbles, good.

Elizabeth: And not be scared.

Mrs. Kingston: And not be scared. What else is happening, Naomi?

Naomi: To put her face in the water.

Mrs. Kingston: That was a big step for Sheila, wasn't it?

Mrs. Kingston, the teacher, initiated the discussion by asking a general question about events in the story. As students responded, Mrs. Kingston evaluated their responses by repeating what was said or by the confirmation "good." Also notice the number of times Mrs. Kingston talked as compared to the students. She was in the conversation every other turn.

In another discussion, the students are talking about chapter three of *Island of the Blue Dolphins* (O'Dell, 1960). Again, as you read through the conversation, observe the pattern of discourse that occurred between the teacher and the students.

Mrs. Kingston (teacher): What picture is in your mind? What are you seeing?

Elaine: You see water, and you see brown things in the water.

Mrs. Kingston: Right. So what's the sea otter doing?

Elaine: Playing.

Mrs. Kingston: Playing, lying on its back, cruising around. Lying there looking at the sky.

Thomas: It looks like . . . .

Mrs. Kingston: He's having fun. He's just playing there.

Mrs. Kingston asks a student to read the next few pages.

Mrs. Kingston: So what did they do to the animals?

Kelly: They skinned them.

Mrs. Kingston: Skinned them, took their pelts off. They took all the skin off. Now you've got what lying around there?

Robert: Bones.

Continuing with the I-R-E structure, Mrs. Kingston asks the questions, students respond to the questions, and Mrs. Kingston evaluates their responses. She interjects every other turn, either to confirm a statement or to ask the next question. As you reflect on these two excerpts, one aspect that stands out is the discrepancy between the amount of talking the teacher does and the amount of talking from the students. The students' responses were often limited to one or two words, a phrase at most. Mrs. Kingston, however, extends the comment, asks questions, and provides more information about the text. This pattern of discourse does not lend itself to students constructing and negotiating new understandings. It is as though the knowledge is already with the teacher.

Literature discussion groups characterized by the teacher asking literal level questions and the students responding at the recall level are accurately known as "recitations." The focus is on the content of the material rather than on the students' understandings or interpretations. Almasi (1996) describes the patterns and roles of discourse in recitation models. Students ask few, if any, questions; they respond to the teacher's questions and do not use strategies to develop conversations. The teacher's role is to ask most, if not all, of the questions, to coordinate/determine who speaks, to lead students to a single answer, to offer one's own insights without prompting

Literature discussion groups characterized by the teacher asking literal level questions and the students responding at the recall level are accurately known as "recitations."

students to share their own, and to provide evaluative feedback. Students have little opportunity to explore or examine divergent and alternative interpretations in the recitation model and I-R-E structure of classroom talk.

Response-Centered Discussions

There are other possibilities besides I-R-E and recitation models. One is the response-centered model where the teacher is involved not as a dictator but as a facilitator and scaffolder (Almasi, 1996). The pattern of talk does not have the teacher responding every other turn. Other students' responses and interpretations are a part of the conversation, and the teacher is less evaluative in his or her comments. The structure of the discussion is more like a conversation where multiple ideas are shared and build upon each other. "The responses, though individual and personal, are clarified, altered, strengthened, and enhanced when shared with others, and variety and approximation rather than correctness are the desired outcomes" (Vogt, 1996, p. 182). In these instances, students verbalize more, both in quality and quantity. Their level of understanding increases.

> The structure of the discussion is more like a conversation where multiple ideas are shared and build upon each other.

The next excerpt is from the same group of students. This time they are discussing chapter two from *Mouse and the Motorcycle* (Cleary, 1965). The classroom teacher is not participating, but I am.

Robert: Okay, let's talk more about like chapter two when he found the motorcycle.

Elizabeth: He said it was beautiful.

Clark: Beautiful? It doesn't even get another paint job.

Robert: And it didn't have a siren; it was just some little toy.
    Thought it was real, but it was just a toy.

Elizabeth: Yeah, you never know, he could ride it though.

Kelly: His mother didn't want him to go on the motorcycle because she was worried.

Clark: This motorbike is only—[cut off by Robert]

Robert: Whose mom? Ralph's mom?

Amy (myself): Do any of you have moms who are big worriers?
    Students in the group all say "yes."

Amy: Can you think of a time when your mom has been overly worried about you?

Elizabeth: She worries that if I go right in the front yard where it's really quiet. She won't let me go out there.

Robert: Cause she might think it's a drive-by (makes automatic gun sound).

A significant difference in this discussion is that the students are in control of the direction and what is discussed. As the facilitator, I came into the discussion not searching for answers from the text but rather to encourage students to make personal connections between the story and their own lives. The students' amount of talk is much greater than in the previous discussions with the teacher. The I-R-E structure is not apparent. There are instances when the students question and challenge each other. Moreover, students are able to construct individual interpretations and share them with the larger group. The process of sharing and negotiating meanings signifies that learning and understanding text occurs in socially situated contexts.

Response-centered discussions provide students with the space and opportunities to construct meaning in individual and collective ways. Students and teachers interact with each other and the text to compose negotiated meanings. Through these discussions, students are able to assume various roles, depending on the purpose for the discussion and the social status held within the classroom community.

Authority Within the Circle

Literature discussions and circles are opportunities to discuss and share interpretations of text. When these opportunities are available in our classrooms, we like to think that all of our students are willing participants and that their voices and interpretations are heard. Yet, when we take a closer look at conversations occurring in classroom literature discussions, we notice that some students and teachers seem to have more authority to determine the appropriateness of a response than others do (Flint, 1997).

Where does that sense of authority come from? In discussions that are modeled in the I-R-E format, the initiate-respond-evaluate structure, teachers maintain the authority through the types of questions they ask and their evaluative comments. Students do not have many opportunities in this structure to assume roles different from that of a responder. Consequently, there is not much shared authority among teachers and students. For example, when a student tries to include background experiences into the discussion and the teacher responds with "We don't have time for stories," the teacher sends a clear message that she is in charge of the discussion and relating personal experiences is not appropriate. Additionally, questions that are "known-answer" and factual also assist teachers in maintaining authority. There is one answer, and the teacher usually knows what the answer is and where it can be located. Authority then is granted to the participant, most often the teacher, who can evaluate responses and has a predetermined agenda for the discussion.

> Response-centered discussions provide students with the space and opportunities to construct meaning in individual and collective ways.

Response-centered discussions reflect a sense of shared authority. The teacher is not a director but more of a facilitator. Facilitators do not determine who speaks next or what the topic of conversation should be. There are few "known-answer" questions and evaluative comments. Students contribute their own interpretations and understandings of the text, as opposed to answering factual questions. These experiences and responses are valued aspects of the discussion. At times the discussion centers on the text, but there are also opportunities to bring in personal experiences and background knowledge. Connecting ideas among texts and experiences supports notions of shared authority because there is not a single "right" answer, as in a response to a factual question. Many perspectives and interpretations can be valued and included in the negotiated construction of meaning.

Students who engage in discussions where the authority is shared among participants explore and examine many different conversation roles. These roles include, but are not limited to,

- ❖ acceptor—one who accepts a response as reasonable and appropriate.
- ❖ catalyst—one who initiates a new idea or direction for the conversations.
- ❖ challenger—one who challenges an interpretation.
- ❖ defender—one who justifies or defends an interpretation.
- ❖ evaluator—one who evaluates responses.
- ❖ inquisitor—one who questions ideas or wonders.
- ❖ speculator—one who considers or deliberates a response.

The discourse roles reflect how participants view themselves within the classroom. Students with confidence, social adeptness, and competence in reading (according to others) generally have opportunities to evaluate and challenge; whereas, students less confident in their abilities assume more acceptor roles (Flint, 1997). Opportunities to assume the different roles greatly depend on whether ideas and interpretations are considered to be valid and are contributions to the discussion.

Let's return to our students in the discussion about chapter two of *Mouse and the Motorcycle* (Cleary, 1965). In that excerpt we can observe Robert and Kelly as catalysts. Robert brings up talking more about Ralph finding the motorcycle, and Kelly addresses the idea that his mom was worried. Clark is one who evaluates responses. He challenges Elizabeth's comment by saying, "Beautiful? It doesn't even get another paint job." Elizabeth assumes an acceptor role by agreeing with Robert's comment about the motorcycle being a toy.

Opportunities to assume the different roles greatly depend on whether ideas and interpretations are considered to be valid and are contributions to the discussion.

Robert also questioned whose mom was being talked about, "Whose mom? Ralph's mom?" As the discussion continued, Clark emerged as one who assumed a greater sense of authority over the text than Elizabeth did. Robert and Kelly maintained some of their authority by initiating new ideas to discuss.

Shared authority in literature discussions contributes to greater meaning construction and understanding of texts. Students have opportunities to challenge, disagree with, accept, or question the ideas of their peers and initiate their own ideas. Through these various discourse roles, students are able to negotiate and determine the validity of multiple perspectives and responses.

Ways to Encourage Shared Authority in Literature Circles

Increasing shared authority is a significant aspect to effective discussions. Encouraging students to accept more diverse discourse roles, considering the types of questions asked during a discussion, and thinking about your instructional stance for a discussion are all possibilities for increasing shared authority. The more opportunity students have to assume roles beyond the responder role, the greater the likelihood for them to become critical, reflective readers. As they read and discuss important issues presented in the text, students explore notions of persuasion and debate. These rhetorical skills help them to understand the subtleties of text.

Questions are critical to the success of your discussions. The more interpretive and applicative in nature your questions, the more insightful your students will be in reading the story. These types of questions provide students with opportunities to venture a response or interpretation. Interpretive questions encourage students to connect background experience and knowledge with current texts. Broadening the discussion to honor and validate the students' experiences increases shared authority by recognizing that each student may bring to the discussion important and valuable contributions.

> The stance adopted for the discussion also contributes to the accessibility to different roles.

The stance adopted for the discussion also contributes to the accessibility to different roles. When a predominately efferent stance is adopted, a student is less likely to assume catalyst and inquisitor roles because of the focus on text-based responses. When students and teachers adopt a predominately aesthetic stance towards the texts, more risks in offering diverse and alternative interpretations are taken. The multiple perspectives brought to a discussion encourage sharing of authority.

Concluding Remarks

Examining the types of discussion structures and how students and teachers participate in those discussions is important to composing meaningful literature circles. Most of the examples in this chapter come from a fourth grade classroom, but certainly the ideas can be extended to any grade level. Kindergarten students in discussions that are in the *initiate, respond, evaluate* structure will quickly learn that one- or two-word responses suffice for the answer. Sixth graders exposed to this type of discussion structure for most of their education generally do not engage in the conversation at a level required for insightful thinking.

Understanding not only the structure of the literature circles but also the various discourse roles students and teachers can assume is also critical. Students reveal these roles in their responses and comments to the teacher and to each other. Their own levels of social status and reading abilities seem to contribute to their abilities and willingness to challenge or accept peers' responses as valid and adding to the discussion. Issues of authority also emerge as salient aspects of discussions, and discovering ways to increase levels of shared authority may lead to discussions that are insightful and meaningful.

Students reveal these roles in their responses and comments to the teacher and to each other.

Literature Circles with Emerging Readers and Writers

Young learners enter the world of school, and these events take on more significance as they embark upon learning to read and write in conventional ways.

Children engage and participate in literacy events even before they begin formal schooling. How many of us are able to relate a story or two about a young child writing a grocery list, taking a meal order as a waitress or waiter, or "reading" a favorite bedtime story? These actions and behaviors are the beginnings of literacy development. Young learners enter the world of school, and these events take on more significance as they embark upon learning to read and write in conventional ways. The ways in which we structure our literacy program, including our literature circles, in the primary grades can greatly influence the attitudes and motivations our students have towards literature and reading.

- How do you structure literature discussions in your classroom?
- What do you do before the discussion, during, and after?
- How do you engage kindergarteners/first graders in meaningful discussions?

Kindergarten/First Grade Classrooms

Our kindergarten and first grade classrooms are brimming with children's literature, environmental print, and opportunities to engage in purposeful literacy activities. We have library corners, writers' tables, and places to draw and act out our favorite characters and events. The walls are full of children's representations and artifacts, drawings, stories, and other such pieces of communication. We make conscious decisions about the types of stories on our shelves, hoping to make connections to math, science, and social studies. We engage in many literacy-based events and activities throughout the day, all moving towards developing "literate thinkers that shape decisions of tomorrow" (Langer, 1995, p.1).

Too often we find our kindergarten and first grade classrooms under siege. The pressure is enormous on the students, teachers, administrators, and parents to learn conventional reading behaviors. Our students spend more time practicing reading skills than they do listening to, reading, and talking about stories and connections to the stories (McGee, 1995). I am not suggesting that learning to read is not a priority in these classrooms, but perhaps more opportunities to respond and talk about quality literature will strengthen children's language development and "provide them with a pool of implicit literary understandings to use in their own reading and writing" (McGee, 1995, p. 106).

Our students spend more time practicing reading skills than they do listening to, reading, and talking about stories and connections to the stories (McGee, 1995).

One significant aspect of reading programs in kindergarten and first grade is read-aloud story time. Reggie Routman (1994) talks about the importance of reading to children: "reading aloud is seen as the single most influential factor in young children's success in learning to read" (p. 32). We know that young students benefit from increased vocabulary, better listening skills, and increased levels of comprehension when engaged in regular story-time opportunities. This is not only true of kindergarten and first grade but is true for all students. It is just that our curriculums and schedules get more and more hurried; we seem to have less time for read-aloud time in the upper grades. Even as adults, we often enjoy hearing stories and poems read to us. One of the most frequent comments I receive as a seminar speaker is that the participants love hearing all the new stories I read.

Story time in the kindergarten/first grade classroom is rarely a quiet activity. Young students are excited about listening to the story and eagerly want to contribute their interpretations and understandings to the larger group. As we consider this opportunity to talk about text with students, it is important that we do not ask too many questions, have too many activities, or focus on too many vocabulary words.

Dissecting a story to cover all of the skills and concepts expected for these young students can ruin the best story and eliminate the pleasures and joy from hearing a story. Our goal in reading stories to students should be to establish a forum for them to share their reactions and experiences. They should be encouraged to explore some of their half-formed and tentative ideas and connections.

Strategies for Engaging in Discussions in the Primary Grades

<u>Prior to Reading</u>

There are a number of possible actions to consider as you plan your read-aloud storytime. Some occur before the reading, others during, and still others after the reading event. Two actions that occur before you read the story to the children are addressed in chapter two—selecting appropriate literature and identifying the composition of the group. Before you even begin the story reading and discussions, you should select literature that will stimulate conversations. This can be daunting with so many selections to choose from. Many times our young readers want to hear their favorites, whether it is one that has stood the test of time and is a classic, such as *Blueberries for Sal* (McCloskey, 1948) and *Madeline* (Bemelmans, 1977), or are recent favorites like *Officer Buckle and Gloria* (Rathman, 1995) and *My Little Sister Ate One Hare* (Grossman, 1996). Refer to the section on reading materials in chapter two for resources to assist you in making decisions and choices. Reading old favorites and new titles should invite young students' participation and involvement with books to challenge and support their thinking and development.

While it is possible to have conversations and discussions with the whole class, the quality of the discussion increases when the group is smaller, say six or eight students. With the smaller group size, students least likely to volunteer a response may be encouraged to do so. The intimacy of the group supports tentative and hesitant voices to emerge. McGee (1995) also suggests that children seem to listen more attentively when the group is smaller. As mentioned in chapter two, having diversity within the group is important. Students benefit from hearing ideas and interpretations from all of their peers, not just those in the same reading or language ability. The group composition should be flexible to include students from various backgrounds and abilities.

A third action to consider before starting the story-time event and discussion is that you will want to preview and read the literature selection. As you preview the story, a number of possibilities emerge. You may want to reflect on your own reactions and feelings to the story or identify those aspects of the story that you think your students

> Our goal in reading stories to students should be to establish a forum for them to share their reactions and experiences.

might find difficult to understand (particularly concepts you believe they have few experiences with). Noticing places where you may want to stop and invite students' responses is a possibility. Additionally, you may want to generate two or three questions to begin the conversation. These questions should be interpretive in nature and ask the students to focus on the significance of the story.

Imagine reading *I Wish I Were a Butterfly* (Howe, 1987) to a group of emerging readers. The story addresses self-esteem when the littlest cricket in the pond does not want to make music because the frog told him he was the ugliest creature ever seen. The cricket believed him and wished to be a beautiful, glistening butterfly. Other creatures in the pond tried to convince the cricket that he had his own beauty, but it is a spider that calls him a beautiful friend and causes feelings of ugliness to fade. What are some places you might want to stop and talk, or what are some possible questions to consider? Perhaps a question asking students to relate a time when they have been called something that was unpleasant or not true will begin a relevant discussion for the story. How did the experience make the student feel?

Encouraging students to share their ideas during the story creates an environment that supports the idea that learning is a social endeavor and that we utilize language as a tool for thinking.

The before actions set the stage for meaningful discussions. Many times setting the stage includes asking students to make predictions about the characters, the setting, and the theme. Building students' background knowledge and inviting personal connections provide them with a framework to understand the themes and concepts of the story.

Reading the Story

While reading the story, students often have comments and responses to contribute. Encouraging students to share their ideas during the story creates an environment that supports the idea that learning is a social endeavor and that we utilize language as a tool for thinking. Stopping the story to discuss areas of the text that may be difficult or problematic provides opportunities for students to explore and examine more closely the ideas presented in the text. As you and the students discuss and talk about particular aspects of the story, the dialogue can help students "piece together the larger picture" (Barrentine, 1996, p. 56). Students begin to understand the structure of the story as well as some of the more embedded insights.

With *I Wish I Were a Butterfly* (Howe, 1987), you might address the emotion of envy and how it is a natural desire to want to be somebody or something else. A couple of key questions might be "Has there ever been a time when you wished you were somebody else?" and "How do you think the butterfly is going to convince the cricket that he is also very special and important?" Students will naturally want to talk about times they have experienced envy or jealousies in their lives.

Discussing aspects of text while you are reading the story enables you to capitalize on "teachable moments." Teachable moments include aspects of the genre, literary elements, or roles of authors and illustrators (McGee, 1995). Students will bring up ideas and issues that you may not have considered, and there may be times while you are reading the story that an idea or a "teachable moment" surfaces. Providing opportunities to interact during the reading event creates a context for shared meaning-making.

After the Story

The general guidelines for including a discussion aspect to your story time can be thought of as possible structure for an activity already occurring in the classroom.

Once the story is concluded, the follow-up questions signal the goals and direction for the discussion. Again, you want to consider questions that lend themselves to multiple responses, ones that are interpretive in nature. Remember that the instructional stance that you enter with is generally the same stance students adopt as they engage in the discussion. So if the focus of your follow-up questions is literal and factual in design, you are encouraging students to read and engage in the discussion with a predominately efferent stance. The intention is to recall information. Conversely, if your questions are designed to allow for multiple perspectives and responses, then students are encouraged to read with a predominately aesthetic stance. The focus is on the connections students construct between their own experiences and the text. Reflecting on the *I Wish I Were a Butterfly* (Howe, 1987) story experience, follow-up questions might include

- What is something or someone you wish you could be?
- What is it about the person or animal that you like; in other words, why do you want to be like him or her?
- What are your special qualities that make you who you are?
- Does this story remind you of other stories you have heard or experiences you have had?"

The general guidelines for including a discussion aspect to your story time can be thought of as possible structure for an activity already occurring in the classroom. The interaction helps students not only to understand the various aspects of the text but also to become more reflective in their thinking. They can hear others' responses and discover ways to connect ideas and interpretations to construct new meanings.

Many times related activities follow a story time or discussion. Our emerging readers and writers are eager to draw and write variations of the story. Encourage students to represent their understandings in drawings and written text. Young students will often draw their favorite scenes or write about their favorite parts of the text. These initial understandings are important as students become more and more comfortable exploring embedded insights and subtleties of text. Examples of young students' drawings for *I Wish I Were a Butterfly* (Howe, 1987) exemplify their understandings and connections between the text and their own experiences.

Composing Literature Circles: Another Example

Now that you have a framework for creating literature discussions with young readers, let's consider *Starring First Grade* (Cohen, 1985) as another possibility for an engaging and interactive discussion. You have established your group and have decided to adopt a predominately aesthetic instructional stance towards the text. In thinking about your stance, you determined that you want students to examine issues of conflict and how to resolve them.

In preparing for the discussion, identify places in the text that you want to talk more about with the students. Perhaps you want to begin with a prediction question about what the story is going to be about with a title like *Starring First Grade*. Elicit students' comments about times when they have performed in front of their families, the class, or larger audiences. You might want to identify those aspects of the text that you had a personal reaction to. For example, you might have an experience of fighting with a sibling or best friend that you can share. You might also talk about how hard it is for you to select students to do something special in the classroom. Throughout the story encourage students to bring in their own understandings and interpretations of the text.

Respond to the direction that your students are interested in pursuing.

After the story is read, continue with a discussion. Having students relate personal experiences and connections to the story contributes to increased reading comprehension. It is important to remain flexible and to not overly control the discussion. Use good judgement when balancing the amount of teacher talk with student talk. Respond to the direction that your students are interested in pursuing. These directions are often insightful and thought provoking and lead to new understandings of the text and the world around them.

As part of the follow-up, you may want students to complete various activities, such as those on pages 38 and 39. Having students pair up and work collaboratively on the first activity provides additional opportunities for them to talk and use language as a tool for constructing meaning. Once students have completed the activity sheets, bringing them together to share their ideas and solutions provides further material for discussion.

Things We Fight About

Every day, most of us either hear others fight about something, or we fight about something ourselves. What we fight about can be big, like a conflict on the playground, or very, very small, like a conflict over cleaning our rooms.

Work with a partner and brainstorm what each of the following groups of people might fight about.

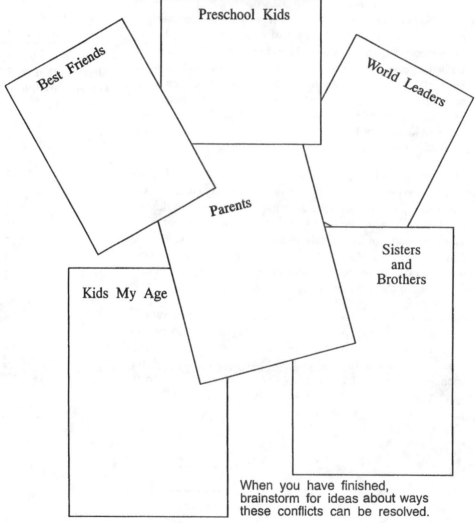

When you have finished, brainstorm for ideas about ways these conflicts can be resolved.

Name _____ Date_____

Book Title _____

SPOTLIGHT ON YOU

Think of one of your favorite parts of the story. Draw a picture of **yourself** in this part of the story. Tell what **you** would do if **you** were a character in this story.

_____

_____

_____

_____

_____

Concluding Remarks

Emerging readers and writers in kindergarten and first grade are enthusiastic and engaging participants in literature circles and discussions. They bring to the event a sense of wonder and excitement. These primary classrooms are filled with literature and children's work that assist them in construct understandings of text and the world around them. As these young readers participate in story time and discussions, there are some general guidelines to help structure the event.

The guidelines for engaging in literature discussions in primary classrooms include identifying high quality literature and realizing that many times your students will want to hear the same story again and again. Revisiting stories is important because we become comfortable with some aspects but gain something new each time. Another step in setting up the discussion is to preview the text to locate points of interest and possible interaction. You also want to establish the group membership, taking into consideration strengths and weaknesses of your students. Composing heterogeneous and flexible groups provides students with opportunities to learn from all of their peers.

Reading the story and encouraging students to interact with each other, you, and the text supports the notion that we learn a great deal in socially situated contexts. The questions and dialogue you have with students helps them to understand text in systematic rather than idiosyncratic ways (Barrentine, 1996). Furthermore, completing the story reading event with a possible activity that highlights students' understandings through drawing and/or written text emphasizes students' abilities to construct sophisticated and insightful interpretations of text.

The questions and dialogue you have with students helps them to understand text in systematic rather than idiosyncratic ways (Barrentine, 1996).

Discovering Texts with Independent Readers and Writers

Literature circles in grades two to six should be a significant aspect of the language arts curriculum. Students in these grades are, for the most part, functional and independent readers. They are reading a variety of genres, often connected to thematic inquiry cycles and units. The discussions students engage in can be enlightening. They provide opportunities to explore and examine the motivations of authors and illustrators. Students can discover subtle messages often embedded within the text.

Recall the group of fourth graders in chapter three who were discussing *Mouse and the Motorcycle* (Cleary, 1965). In one of their discussions, Kelly brought up the idea that the author would not write about the mouse stealing money from a table in the lobby because, as Kelly said, "Well, this is like a child's book. I don't think there would be robbing in it." Elaine adds to that statement by saying, "I don't think they'll want children trying to do the same thing." For Kelly, Elaine, and the others, uncovering such insights occurred when they were presented with the opportunity to talk about the story in a forum that was directed and ultimately controlled by them. It is through these dialogues and discussions that students are able to make sense of the world around them and their place within the world.

- How do you structure literature discussions in your classroom, particularly when students are reading different texts?
- How do you engage second through sixth graders in meaningful discussions?

Whole Group Literature Selections

The whole class literature discussion format is most common in classrooms where a teacher is beginning to move away from a basal reading series or the text is one that has been determined as a "core literature" selection—one that all students in that grade level should be exposed to. A single text may also be used in classrooms where the text is the center of a specified unit or theme, such as *Sarah, Plain and Tall* (MacLachlan, 1987) for a unit on pioneer life.

Similar to composing literature discussion groups and circles among emerging readers, whole group literature selections with students who read independently should be carefully crafted so that the discussions are thought provoking and meaningful. These literature discussions are based on the same steps that teachers take to establish literature discussions with emerging readers. It is important to select texts that address human experience and concerns. Again, referring to references such as *The Reading Teacher's* "Teachers' Choices" awards for the previous year or *Book List's* collection of award winning selections provides excellent titles to choose from. Deciding on the text to read and talk about is critical to the success of the discussion.

Additionally, group composition is critical. Often in these grades, there is more distance between the strengths and weaknesses of students. You will have students in the second grade who read well above grade level, and you will have students in the fifth grade struggling with text at the second grade level. There will be students who socialize well and work well with peers; others will prefer to work by themselves and seem not to contribute much in group discussions. Groups that have a range of student strengths and weaknesses allow for more social interaction, and students come to realize there is much to be learned from peers. Creating a grid like the one described in chapter two can be useful in arranging groups.

Points of interest or areas that may be problematic to the readers should also be identified before reading and discussing the story. There may be aspects of the text that need further clarification because

> It is important to select texts that address human experience and concerns.

your students have not had the experiences to help them construct understandings. Composing and asking a few interpretive questions pushes the students' thinking to help them make connections among ideas, experiences, and texts. While the questions and points of interest raised by the teacher may only be suggestions for a possible direction, they help to focus discussions when necessary.

What about other formats and structures, though, that encourage students to construct connections, make more decisions about what they read, and develop ways of interacting with the story?

Managing Multiple Literature Circles

Teachers implementing literature circles as a significant aspect of the reading program may have more than one text as the source for discussions. In these situations, students may select their own texts to read, decide which group to participate in, or determine the course of action to take with a particular text. There are many different activities and discussions occurring at the same time. In what ways can a teacher facilitate and encourage students to construct meaningful discussions of texts when students are taking many different pathways?

> Inquiry cycles are a part of a curricular framework that honors students' natural tendencies as inquirers.

One possibility for organizing discussions is to have students conduct inquiry cycles in areas of personal interest. Within such inquiry cycles, students are reading and discussing multiple texts in a variety of genres. Below is a detailed look at how to establish inquiry cycles and text sets in your classroom, leading to authentic discussions about texts. Examples for a discussion based on a narrative text and one on an expository text are interwoven within the descriptions.

Development of Inquiry Cycles and Text Sets

Inquiry cycles and text sets enable students to explore and examine a variety of interests. Inquiry cycles are a part of a curricular framework that honors students' natural tendencies as inquirers. We all know the two-, three-, and four-year olds who ask "why" questions continuously. For them, discovering and investigating the world around them is who they are and how they go about learning. This natural tendency is systematically reduced as children enter school and begin their school careers. There becomes a single answer to focus on, a single approach to a problem. Children no longer pursue their interests but those of the teacher or curriculum planners. Inquiry cycles are one way to reverse that trend.

Inquiry Questions

Asking questions is the first step in an inquiry cycle. Inquiry questions should be based on an authentic desire to learn about something. Short, Harste, and Burke (1996) identify three sources of knowledge that inquiry cycle questions stem from. These sources include personal and social knowledge, knowledge systems (history, politics, ecology, etc.) and alternative perspectives, and sign systems (art, music, movement, language, etc.). A teacher can not know exactly the direction students will take with particular ideas or concepts because students bring to the inquiry their own experiences and knowledge.

As students pursue questions that are significant to their own lives, they utilize knowledge systems and sign systems as tools for exploring and examining their questions. The focus is on inquiry. Encouraging students to construct their own questions complements issues of ownership and authenticity. When students are in charge of creating questions for the inquiry, they are more likely to be engaged.

In one example, let us imagine that a group of students (ages 7–9) have finished reading *Bein' with You This Way* (Nikola-Lisa, 1994). After the story, they became intrigued and interested in why people look different. In exploring differences, they pose the following questions: "How do people feel who are different from those around them?" "Why do some people have freckles?" "Why do we have different-colored skins?" and "Where do different names come from?" The broadness of these questions enables the students to bring into the discussions and inquiry their own perspectives and interests. These questions are only a sampling of the possibilities.

A group of upper-grade students (ages 9–12) completed *Number the Stars* (Lowry, 1989) and were interested in further understanding the Holocaust and the devastating effects on people. Possible questions to explore included, "How did the Holocaust start?" "Why did people let it happen?" and "Why are people still prejudiced today?" "How can we stop people from being prejudiced?" The scope of these questions provides students with multiple directions to explore—past, present, and future.

Text Sets

Once questions are posed, the next step in an inquiry cycle is to select texts that complement or suggest alternative perspectives to the themed questions. This collection is known as a text set. Text sets can range in number from two to many and reflect a variety of sign systems (print and non-print materials). A teacher's knowledge of

> A teacher can not know exactly the direction students will take with particular ideas or concepts because students bring to the inquiry their own experiences and knowledge.

possible sources and students' interest in the theme intersect as text sets are put together in a variety of ways. Short, Harste, and Burke (1996) state that "learning is a process of searching for patterns that connect" (p. 537). When students read and discuss texts that are in some way related, their understandings of each text change. Students begin to search for possible connections and develop strategies to bring ideas together in meaningful discussions. Short, Harste, and Burke (1996) have also identified criteria to use when putting together text sets for a variety of purposes.

❖ Degree of familiarity—some of the books should connect closely to the students' expectations and background experiences. Others in the set should present alternative perspectives to challenge assumptions.

❖ Range of genres and materials—materials in the text set should include poetry, fiction, and informational texts, as well as songs, maps, articles, posters, etc. Alternative sign systems encourage students to take different perspectives.

❖ Knowledge systems—texts can include a range of disciplines, such as history, ecology, science.

❖ Cultural perspectives and language—texts sets should reflect a range of cultural perspectives, including gender, race, socioeconomic status, ethnicity, and race. Try to identify books written by cultural insiders rather than books about the country or group of people.

❖ Difficulty of text—the set should represent a range of difficulty in reading. Some are used for browsing or reference while others are to be read in their entirety.

> When students read and discuss texts that are in some way related, their understandings of each text change.

For the inquiry on differences, the following texts may be possibilities for a text set: *Bright Eyes, Brown Skin* (Hudson & Ford, 1990), *My Best Friend* (Hutchins, 1993), *Freckle Juice* (Blume, 1971), *Chrysanthemum* (Henkes, 1996), *Every Living Thing* (Rylant, 1985), *I Wish I Were a Butterfly* (Howe, 1987), and *Molly's Pilgrim* (Cohen, 1983).

The inquiry on the Holocaust can produce this list as a possible text set: *Against All Odds: Holocaust Survivors and the Successful Lives They Made in America* (Helmreich, 1993), *I Never Saw Another Butterfly: Children's Drawings and Poems from Terezin Concentration Camp, 1942–1944* (Volavkova, 1978), *The Devil's Arithmetic* (Yolen, 1988), *We Remember the Holocaust* (Adler, 1989), *Daniel's Story* (Matas, 1993), and information from any number of museums and institutes (U.S. Holocaust Memorial Museum, Holocaust Education and Memorial, and Anne Frank Institute of Philadelphia).

Considering the criteria outlined above, the selected texts reflect students' background experiences, depict a range of genres and difficulty, and represent different knowledge systems. The texts also include diverse cultural perspectives on the issue of difference and the Holocaust.

Discussing Texts in Inquiry Cycles

Text sets compose the heart of literature circles in inquiry cycles. These texts are discussed in different forums. Sometimes students will each read one or two of the selections and come together to share their texts with the group, looking for commonalties and differences. Students retell the story and share what the book was about in relation to the theme. As retellings are shared, students begin to make connections and discover differences among the texts. The similarities and differences can be in relation to contents as well as structures of the texts. At other times, students read the range of texts and then share their own understandings and connections across the entire set. The questions students pose about their particular theme should be reference points and do not necessarily need to be answered by a particular source in the text set. In most cases, the questions are broad in nature and only serve to focus the direction of the inquiry and discussion.

> **The questions students pose about their particular theme should be reference points and do not necessarily need to be answered by a particular source in the text set.**

The classroom environment during literature discussions of text sets is noisy and lively. Students are in their various groups, and each group may be at a different point in their inquiry. Some students are reading, some are discussing, and others are engaged in further research and questions. The teacher's role in this environment is to facilitate the learning process and provide models of effective and thought provoking discussions. Within the model, conversations should occur about how to enter the discussion, how to listen to peers, and how to construct negotiated meanings. Sometimes teachers will have students role-play various discussions with follow-up conversation on the aspects of the discussion that worked well and aspects that did not work so well. Hanging charts of possible statements provides them with an easy reference while they are engaged in a discussion (Routman, 1994).

I'd like to add…

I agree because…

I don't understand what you mean…

I'm confused…

I'd like to expand on what you said…

Once students become comfortable leading their own discussions, you can determine which of the many groups to join on that day. Listening to the students examine the many facets of a text set provides you with knowledge and information about your students as inquirers and readers. You can observe group dynamics or students' contributions (more will be discussed in the assessment chapter). Making the transition from a director to a facilitator is sometimes a difficult challenge but is well worth the effort. You can continue to model good questioning and response techniques by following the lead and direction students have determined. The authenticity of students' initial inquiry questions serves to guide meaningful discussions. Students gain a sense of ownership and empowerment as the teacher participates in but does not dominate the conversations.

Reflecting on our examples, the inquiry group on difference focuses on how and why people want to look different. In particular, the texts *Freckle Juice* (Blume, 1971) and *I Wish I Were a Butterfly* (Howe, 1987) address the idea that people or creatures are rarely happy with what or who they are. Some students reflect on their own family members changing hair color, hairstyles, and weight and adding tattoos. Others talk about how they wished they could change something about themselves. The discussion evolves into wondering why people are not satisfied with their own appearances, and further inquiry questions are conceived. Issues about how the media portrays certain people and stereotypes emerge.

Students inquiring about the Holocaust discuss why it occurred and what is happening today in various parts of the world. They read and discuss aspects of the Holocaust from other points of view and confront important issues related to this time in our history. In reading both narrative and informational texts, students are struck by the numbers of people sent to the concentration camps. They search multiple sources to verify the facts.

During the discussion, students engage in a strategy known as RBL—*reading between the lines* (Mazzoni & Gambrell, 1996). Questions are asked which encourage students to critically examine texts for authors' intentions, hidden agendas, and missing information. Sample questions adapted from Mazzoni and Gambrell:

- Who wrote this? What group does the author belong to?
- When you read this text, are there any places that confuse you? Describe.
- Is there any information that you think the author left out? Why do you think the author left this information out?

> **The authenticity of students' initial inquiry questions serves to guide meaningful discussions.**

Students talk about their responses to these questions, using the text to support a point. A strategy such as this encourages students to be more critical of the information they read and to identify dissenting points of view.

The two illustrations focus not on the teacher but rather on the students. In both situations, it is possible for the teacher to "step out" of the discussion and let students facilitate their own discussions. By stepping out, teachers may or may not be present, depending on the group and the goals for the students. If the teacher is present, he or she is a participant, not a director. If teachers choose not to be present, students can manage their own discussions quite successfully. Students are genuinely engaged in discovering answers to their own questions.

Given the chance to facilitate their own discussions, students adopt the stance that is most appropriate for the task and text.

Stepping out of the discussion also contributes to students adopting personal stances that make the most sense for the text. As they read stories, texts, and other materials, the stance for the narrative selections should be one that is predominately aesthetic in nature. Students want to talk about the "lived through" aspects of the story. This will encourage further connections and points of interest. While facilitating these discussions, a teacher should be careful not to bring into the discussion an efferent stance perspective and have students identify discrete basic comprehension material.

Conversely, when reading and discussing expository text, the adopted stance will probably be one that is predominately efferent in nature. Students are interested in locating details and facts to support their responses in strategies such as RBL. Given the chance to facilitate their own discussions, students adopt the stance that is most appropriate for the task and text.

Further Engagements in Inquiry Cycles and Discussions

Similar to literature discussions with emerging readers, follow-up activities may help to bring various ideas and concepts together for students engaged in inquiry cycles. These types of activities should be optional to students and utilized in meaningful and productive ways. Possibilities for follow-up for the two examples are included on the next three pages. As students complete these activities, there should be opportunities for the groups to reconvene and share interpretations and responses to these activity sheets.

I Like My . . .

In the end, Andrew was happy with himself, even without freckles. Think about yourself for a minute. What are all the things you like about yourself? Write your thoughts in the space below. Use these questions to help you think.

- What do I like about the way I look?
- What do I like about the way I act?
- What do I like about the way I feel?
- What makes me who I am?

Holocaust Tile

Directions: Students from across the United States created handpainted tiles that expressed their feelings about the Holocaust. More than 3,000 of these tiles are mounted on the Wall of Remembrance in the U.S. Holocaust Memorial Museum in Washington, D.C. In the space provided below, create a tile that represents your feelings about the Holocaust.

Tough Times

Directions: Contributing to Hitler's rise were many economic, political, and social conditions, such as large numbers of people being unemployed, resentment for conditions following Germany's loss of World War I, and widespread religious prejudice. In the space provided below, identify as many of these conditions as possible.

Economic Conditions

_____   _____

_____   _____

Political Conditions

_____   _____

_____   _____

Social Conditions

_____   _____

_____   _____

Identify any of these conditions that exist in the U.S. today by placing a check beside them. Then list additional economic, political, and social conditions that exist in the U.S. today.

Economic Conditions

_____   _____

_____   _____

_____   _____

Political Conditions

_____   _____

_____   _____

Social Conditions

_____   _____

_____   _____

Place each of the conditions on a scale from 1 (low) to 10 (high) in level of importance. You can number the conditions and place the number before the appropriate item.

Literature Discussion Logs/Response Journals

Perhaps one of the most common activities to include during an inquiry cycle and literature discussion is a literature discussion log or response journal. Students record their thoughts, feelings, questions, and wonderings while reading the story, and each brings this document to the discussions as a source of ideas to talk about. The journals serve as learning tools for students as they discover concepts and ideas in literature.

Reading and writing are two interwoven processes students actualize to construct understandings about the world around them. Writing in literature discussion logs or response journals contributes to students' reflective thinking. "If we believe that it is through language that our thinking is developed, the very *act* of writing may help us come to understand both what we already know and what we have yet to learn" (Raphael and Hiebert, 1996, p. 228). As students write entries in their journals, they reflect on the story and possible connections to the story and construct new interpretations of the text. The literature logs become sources for extended writing whereby students can revisit, reflect, and reconsider earlier ideas as new understandings emerge from discussions.

> **Writing in literature discussion logs or response journals contributes to students' reflective thinking.**

There are many ways of responding to literature through written text. Raphael and Hiebert (1996) identify three very common types of responses for literature journals—comprehension-oriented entries, evaluative entries, and personal responses. Students use their journals to improve comprehension by recording observations and speculations. Simple retellings and summaries provide students with information from the text to share with others in literature circles. They use speculation-oriented thinking to ask questions and make predictions about what may occur next in the story. The comprehension-oriented entries help students reflect on and articulate some of their understandings of the story, including instances where comprehension may have failed to occur.

Evaluative entries and personal responses enable students to evaluate the story and their own understandings. These responses build the bridge between comprehension of text and personal reactions. In evaluative responses, students evaluate various components of the text and provide examples for such opinions. Personal responses reveal how students are internalizing themes of the story and how the story relates to their own experiences and understandings. Students will often connect these ideas to other stories and texts with similar concepts or themes. Recalling Short, Harste, and Burke's (1996) comment that learning is about finding patterns and connections, teachers find that personal responses in literature journals provide patterns and connections. Literature logs promote a range of thinking from text-based ideas to personal interpretations. Entries can be webs, sketches, charts, favorite quotes, and diagrams, as well as written reflections (Short, Harste, & Burke, 1996).

The different ways to respond in writing promote engagement and motivation. Deciding on the type of entry provides students with a sense of ownership. They can utilize their journals during discussions to spark new ideas and further commentary. The journals are generally a place for students to explore and focus on their own interpretations and reactions, and "concentrate on thinking and reflecting, not on grammar and spelling" (Short, Harste, & Burke, 1996, p. 468).

Concluding Remarks

Literature discussions with independent readers can be exciting. Students often bring up ideas and concepts that are thought provoking and meaningful as they discover the world around them. Text selection, group composition, and previewing the text are important components to conducting literature discussions with the whole class. In many instances, however, literature discussions with independent readers are often part of inquiry cycles.

Not all texts satisfy the questions, but through the connections and interpretations, students may identify possible answers and conceive of new directions to proceed.

Inquiry cycles are opportunities for students to inquire about topics and themes of interest. Students compose their own inquiry questions, and with the assistance of the teacher, text sets are created. They read one or two of the texts or all of the texts in the set and conduct literature discussions, searching for commonalties, differences, and possible responses to their questions. Not all texts satisfy the questions, but through the connections and interpretations, students may identify possible answers and conceive of new directions to proceed. Teachers involved in the discussions are participants and facilitators rather than directors and leaders. A teacher's voice and responses should not overpower the ideas and interpretations of the students. However, it is the responsibility of a teacher to continue modeling good questioning and responding strategies.

Finally, follow-up activities and writing events help to pull ideas and interpretations together in meaningful ways. The activities should reflect students' interests and make sense to the literature discussion and inquiry cycle. Literature discussion logs and response journals are common practices among students in grades two to six. Students can respond in a variety of ways, from comprehension-oriented responses to evaluative responses to personal responses. The range of responses enables students to construct meanings from multiple perspectives and bring to the discussions new insights to consider.

Literature Circles and Assessment

Literature discussions and circles enable students and teachers to share new insights and interpretations of texts in classroom environments. Discussions vary, depending on the students, texts, teachers, formats, purposes, and goals for the literacy event. The variations among these components also influence the assessment practices and outcomes.

The complexity and diversity of literature discussions create nearly impossible situations for the types of assessment we are more familiar with—report cards and tests. There does not seem to be a place on traditional report cards for "literature circles," yet many students spend a majority of their language arts block of instructional time in such structures. How do teachers go about "grading" discussions? Is it possible to accurately assess students' comprehension of text when interpretations are negotiated among peers?

- In what ways do you assess students as they participate in discussions and literature circles?

Traditional Assessments Do Not Reveal Our Complex Understandings

Our decisions for instruction and assessment are based on what we view as important to being an educated individual (Bisesi & Raphael, 1997). Traditional and standardized forms of assessment are ingrained into our educational system. We administer any number of standardized tests to our students, requiring them to master discrete, isolated skills related to reading and writing. "Predictably, these tests contribute to students' emphasis on performance over learning and teachers' providing instruction on tested skills rather than teaching in ways more consistent with their beliefs about literacy" (Bisesi & Raphael, 1997, p. 184). Students also experience chapter-end tests, spelling tests, vocabulary tests, and informal evaluations during discussions conducted in an I-R-E format in reading and language arts.

Our decisions for instruction and assessment are based on what we view as important to being an educated individual (Bisesi & Raphael, 1997).

Traditional assessment practices evaluate students' knowledge of specific skills and concepts rather than their understandings of the text as related to other experiences and other texts. Tests often focus on main ideas, characters, definitions, and chronological events of the story. In most cases, the tests are multiple choice or single short answer. There is little room for explanation or to better understand a student's thought process for a particular interpretation. The focus is to judge a student's product—to mark, grade, or score—and often has little connection to a teacher's instructional plan (Rhodes & Shanklin, 1993).

This lack of connection to a teacher's instructional plan reflects a misalignment between instruction and assessment. What we assess and evaluate should be what we teach. The alignment of instruction and assessment creates an awareness that what is taught is assessed, and the information gained from the assessment is meaningful and will be utilized in future decisions (Seely, 1994).

For example, a group of sixth grade students engaged in a literature discussion for the story *Walk Two Moons* (Creech, 1994) explored many issues related to family relationships. A chapter-end test asking students to individually identify various details of the story is not aligned with how the story was presented in the classroom. The assessment practices connected to this literature discussion should uncover what students know about participating in such discourse structures as well as what students comprehend from the story and connections to their own experiences and those of their peers. Alignment between instruction and assessment creates an interrelated pathway towards meaning.

Moreover, traditional assessment practices do not reveal the breadth and depth of understanding. Students often bring in their own experiences and other texts to make sense of the story and the world around them. Issues of character motivations, author intentions, and related experiences are generally the sources of conversation. It is important that teachers who have structured their literature discussions to be more than vocalized work sheets not revert to using a form of assessment requiring students to pull out specific details and define particular words from texts.

If Not Chapter-End Tests, Then What?

Our new ways of thinking about literacy development and the social nature of learning embrace new forms of assessment known to most as alternative assessment. Alternative assessment practices range from observations and anecdotal records to checklists, rubrics, and self-evaluations. Guiding principles of alternative assessment practices are outlined in a number of resources (Valencia, 1990; Rhodes & Shanklin, 1993; Routman, 1994; Raphael & Hiebert, 1996). Some of these principles include (a) assess authentic reading and writing events in a variety of contexts, (b) assess products as well as process, (c) view assessment as ongoing and an integral part of the teaching-learning process, (d) emphasize systematic record collection, and (e) involve others in decisions. Assessment should be meaningful, relevant, and further instruction. These guiding principles set the stage for thinking about how assessment practices factor into establishing effective and successful literature discussions.

Assessing authentic reading and writing events reflects the idea of aligning instruction with assessment. If a teacher implements literature discussions to allow for a variety of interpretations, then assessment practices should also value divergent interpretations. Focusing on a student's process as well as the product provides much information on how the student comes to understand particular concepts and the connections being formed. When a teacher attends to a student's thinking process, new insights emerge about the student as a learner. Furthermore, assessment practices that are ongoing and integral aspects of the teaching and learning process are more informative and effective.

The next two principles, systematic recordkeeping and involving others in the process, support the belief that when observations are recorded and not just kept in the teacher's head, decisions are more justifiable and valid. Also when others, including school personnel, parents, and students, are involved in the process, a richer understanding of the student emerges. Students asked to assess their own progress are challenged to reflect on strategies and monitor their own efforts.

> When a teacher attends to a student's thinking process, new insights emerge about the student as a learner.

These few guiding principles of alternative assessment influence the types of assessment practices that make the most sense for literature circles. The practices most useful for literature discussions include observations, group and self-evaluations, and rubrics. These methods reflect the ongoing literacy events, involve others in the process, record both process and product, and occur in a variety of contexts. Moreover, the use of these alternative assessment practices provides you with better understanding of the progress your students are making in reading and writing events.

Observing the Complexities

Observing students is an integral aspect of our role in the classroom. We notice the ways in which our students interact with others and how they construct meanings of texts. Many of us are experts at observation, yet we often fail to acknowledge the wealth of information we are able to obtain through observation. Observations occur in a variety of settings, whether our students are working individually, in pairs, or in groups. The actions and behaviors we pay attention to are determined by the goals and purposes we have for the literacy event. In the case of literature circles, we often want to know how students interact with others in the group and what the content of the discussion is.

> Many of us are experts at observation, yet we often fail to acknowledge the wealth of information we are able to obtain through observation.

Observations can take various forms, but one of the most useful for literature discussions is an anecdotal record. Anecdotal records are dated informal notes teachers write while they are observing students or directly after. These notes are descriptive in nature, recording the significant aspects of the occasion, including strategies used, language development, social skills and abilities, learning styles, and attitudes (Routman, 1994). First attempts at recording your observations may not yield much significant data. You may not know what to focus on and end up with a mixed bag of comments to sort through. Remember that practice results in more meaningful notes. Having confidence and valuing the information you gain will increase the usefulness of the assessment. A sample of an anecdotal form is provided on page 58. This form is generic and can be utilized in many different contexts.

Literature discussion should be examined multidimensionally (Matanzo, 1996). Three dimensions to consider include discussion behaviors, elements of narrative text, and elements of expository text. There are numerous possibilities in these categories, and the chart on page 59 provides a sample of what can be observed and assessed. These possibilities are taken from Matanzo (1996).

Individual Anecdotal Record Form

Run off a stack of these forms and keep them — one for each student in your class — in a three-ring binder. Make your notes right on the appropriate form. When a page is filled up, it can be replaced with a new page and the filled page placed in the student's portfolio. No time is lost transcribing information!

Individual Anecdotal Record

Name _____

Date	Comment

Discussions Behaviors	Narrative Content	Expository Content
Avoid interruptions	Character analysis	Organization of ideas
Take turns	Plot analysis	Effectiveness of examples
Make eye contact	Conflict and resolution	Stereotype analysis
Stay focused on topic	Texts of similar themes	Author's clarity
Question others	Compares works of given author	Accuracy
Project voice	Dialogue effectiveness	Compare text to media
Extend ideas of others	Character motivations	Title appropriateness
Locate support in text		

The elements described for a literature circle provide a framework as you begin to observe and assess students' interactions and behaviors. Developing a checklist is another strategy for effective assessment. The elements you decide to focus on should be appropriate and relevant for your students and for the text. First graders may not focus on the effectiveness of dialogue, but for third and fourth graders, this may be a significant aspect of a story they are reading. Students can assist in creating the list of expectations and behaviors that are appropriate for a checklist. Encouraging students to participate in creating the list promotes empowerment and ownership of the discussion process. Utilizing a form such as the one provided on page 60 is helpful as you begin to identify those aspects of the discussion you want to observe students engaging in.

The elements you decide to focus on should be appropriate and relevant for your students and for the text.

Finding the time to observe and record your observations is difficult at best. You may be thinking about how you can possibly facilitate a literature discussion and take anecdotal notes at the same time. You are right—it is virtually impossible to do both well. Maybe in these cases you will want to step out of the discussion and let students facilitate the conversation. By stepping out and recording your observations, two goals are achieved. One, you no longer control the discussion because you are busy with another task, and two, this other task will provide you with useful and meaningful information to reflect on at a later date. Initially, students may wonder what you are doing and will want to know what you are writing. Sharing some of the positive comments with students may increase their confidence in facilitating and participating in the discussions.

Use this classroom checklist to compile results from individual checklists. Run off enough
copies to accommodate all the students in your class.

Classroom Checklist—Elements of Literature

There are many different management systems teachers have in place for recording their observations. Some use Post-it notes and labels that they later attach to a piece of paper with the student's name. Others utilize three-ring binders with dividers for each student and record the information within each section. Clipboards are also a favorite among teachers and "clipboard cruising" is a common strategy—teachers document their observations as they walk around the room or sit with a group of students. Discovering the system and strategies that work best for you is most important as you begin to incorporate anecdotal records and checklists into your assessment practices.

The benefits of using anecdotal records and checklists outweigh some of the initial difficulties in making the transition. They are useful during parent and student conferences. You can use the information to complete the narrative component of report cards. Observations can also promote reflection on student progress and growth (Routman, 1994). These alternative assessment practices are beneficial when considering students' actions and behaviors in literature discussions.

Group and Self-Assessments

Literature discussions and circles are excellent opportunities for students to reflect on their own progress and process in literacy development. Self-assessments encourage students to think about their own levels of participation and their contributions to the discussion. They reflect on their perceptions of the reading and writing process, literacy instruction, and the strategies used to construct meaning and engage in literature discussions (Rhodes & Shanklin, 1993). Uncovering this information is useful to teachers as they plan and implement discussions in the classroom. A student who reveals that she thinks a good reader is one who reads without mistakes may benefit from being in a group of students who do not necessarily read well orally but construct interesting and insightful responses. How students view themselves as readers and writers and their uses of various strategies may provide new information for your own teaching practices.

Self-assessments can be structured or unstructured as determined by the goals and needs of the assessment. In general, students with less experience in knowing strategies and their own potentials in reading and writing require more structure if the self-assessments are to encourage reflection (Rhodes & Shanklin, 1993). Structured self-assessments often have questions or responses that students check off or answer yes/no. Less structured formats are more open-ended where the students provide information about their own strategies and ideas. Samples of self-assessments are on the following page.

> How students view themselves as readers and writers and their uses of various strategies may provide new information for your own teaching practices.

SELF-EVALUATION

(Adapted from Lapp, Flood, Ranck-Buhr, Van Dyke, & Spacek, 1997)

Name _____

Book Title _____

Date _____

Other group members _____

This is the level I participated at today:

        high   medium   low

This is why I think my participation was at this level._____

_____

What did I do well in the group today? _____

_____

How do I think the group functioned today in the discussion? _____

_____

What did I talk about today?_____

_____

How can I be an even better group member? _____

• •

SELF-EVALUATION

(Adapted from Routman, 1994)

Name _____

Date _____

Book Title _____

What did I do well today (and/or improve on) during group discussions? _____

_____

What do I still need to improve on in group discussions? _____

_____

_____

Group assessments are beneficial to teachers' understandings of what occurred in literature discussions without their presence. In group assessments students complete a form that rates the effectiveness of the group in terms of how well they listened, shared, and responded to each other. As a group, students are asked to rate participation levels, identify a continuing question about the text, and describe aspects of the discussion that worked well and aspects that need further help (Vogt, 1996). Students have opportunities to reflect on the discussion as a whole rather than on individual participation and actions.

Reflection journals are useful tools for fostering reflection and self-assessment. Students have opportunities to clarify some of their thinking and what has, or has not, been learned. Guiding questions may include "What did I do or say in the literature discussion group?" "What am I still wondering about?" and "What do I want to bring up tomorrow to the group?" These journal entries are not corrected or graded, but they are used to spark students' thinking about what they do in discussion groups.

> The pressure of giving grades continues to derail meaningful assessment practices.

Rubrics and Report Cards

Perhaps the most difficult aspect of utilizing alternative assessment practices in our classrooms is that in the majority of school districts, we are still required to reduce all of our knowledge and insights to a single letter grade. The pressure of giving grades continues to derail meaningful assessment practices. We seem to not know how to make sense of our other forms of assessment (e.g., checklists, anecdotal records, self- and group evaluations) when it comes to recording a grade on the report card. One possibility that may help in bringing these documents together is a rubric.

A rubric is an articulated set of criteria established before the activity or project, in this case, before engaging in literature discussions. Rubrics are generally on three- or six-point scales. The more numbers on the scale, the more specific the actions and behaviors are for each number. An illustration of a generalized task rubric is on page 65.

Cooperative Investigations

Group Process Evaluation

Name _____

Group Members _____

Literature Discussion _____

_____

1. Describe how well members participated in the discussion. _____

_____

_____

_____

2. What were the group's strengths? _____

_____

_____

_____

3. What frustrations did the group encounter? _____

_____

_____

_____

4. Did all members of the group participate? _____

5. Did you listen to each other? _____

6. Name two ways in which your group could improve in order to be more effective on your next literature discussion. _____

7. What question does your group still have about the story? _____

_____

_____

_____

Generalized Task Rubric

The generalized task rubric below is a more complex version of the DO-IT-YOURSELF RUBRIC. It can be used as a template from which to build specific elaborated rubrics.

An elaborated rubric can be devised to fit a particular prompt in any subject area by adding specific elements to the categories in the generalized rubric, building both up and down the scale from Score 4 which is the midpoint.

Scores 6 and 5 would be considered high papers, Scores 4 and 3 would be high/low average, and Scores 2 and 1 would be attempts that "need revision" or "need correction." Failure is not part of teaching with a rubric, since the student can always try again.

Generalized Task Rubric

Score 6: *Exemplary Achievement*

Score 5: *Commendable Achievement*

Score 4: *Adequate Achievement*

(demonstrates a general understanding of the major concepts)

Score 3: *Some Evidence of Achievement*

Score 2: *Limited Evidence of Achievement*

Score 1: *Minimal Evidence of Achievement*

Score 0: *No Response*

The criteria for a rubric in literature discussions should encompass both process and product in various contexts. Meeting the criteria may range from consistent behavior (9 out of 10, for example) to inconsistent behavior (5 or fewer out of 10). For literature discussions, you might establish the following criteria as aspects to consider when assessing students' performances:

- Contributes thoughtful responses
- Listens attentively to peers
- Responds to peers' comments
- Refers to literature journal or text to support interpretations
- Reflects on personal experiences
- Knows how to enter the discussion without interrupting

Rubrics can help establish the benchmarks for a particular grade.

These criteria are only a sample and should be negotiated with your students. Again, more involvement from students in assessment practices promotes ownership and empowerment. The criteria for the rubric should be flexible and open to revision as necessary.

Rubrics can help establish the benchmarks for a particular grade. What are the specific actions and behaviors you expect for an "A" or a "C?" The consistency factor for various behaviors can be documented and translated into a letter grade (Routman, 1994).

> A = consistency for all areas
>
> B = consistency for most areas
>
> C = consistency for some areas
>
> D = inconsistency for most areas
>
> F = inconsistency for all areas

Also, reflecting on the other documents—anecdotal records, checklists, and self-reporting strategies—helps to support the judgements made for the rubric and, ultimately, the letter grade.

Concluding Remarks

After planning and implementing literature discussions in your classroom, it is important to also assess students' performances and learning in these discussions. Alternative assessment practices encourage us to rely on multiple sources to document how students apply knowledge in different contexts. These sources not only assess products but also the processes and strategies students actualize to construct meaningful interpretations of texts.

The most efficient and viable forms of alternative assessment for literature discussions are observation—anecdotal records and checklists. Teachers should take opportunities to step out of the discussion and observe from the outside what is occurring among students in discussion groups. Observing and systematically recording students' behaviors and comments help to shape future discussions.

Opportunities for students to engage in self-reporting assessments such as self-evaluations and group evaluations are valuable. These strategies encourage students to reflect on their own behaviors and interpretations in light of what others in the group said and did. Through the self-reporting documents students become more aware of their participation and are helped to refine and extend their repertoires for discussion.

Alternative assessment strategies can be used to document students' growth and progress during literature discussions. Examining and reflecting on the teaching and learning process are critical to constructing meaningful discussions about texts and lead to more complete understandings of our students' literacy development.

Observing and systematically recording students' behaviors and comments help to shape future discussions.

Continuing to Move Forward

Many of the ideas addressed throughout the chapters come together at the same time during a discussion, particularly ideas related to stance, patterns of talk, and assessment.

The challenge was accepted, and now you are ready to implement effective and thought-provoking literature discussions in your classroom. Many ideas, some new and some revisited, were presented in hopes of making the challenge accessible to anyone wanting to try. As these concepts and strategies were shared, it was my intention that literature circles and discussions would become the focal point of your language arts curriculum.

One downfall in reading a book on literature circles is that the concepts must be presented in a linear fashion yet this is not how I believe literature circles are enacted. Many of the ideas addressed throughout the chapters come together at the same time during a discussion, particularly ideas related to stance, patterns of talk, and assessment.

The first three chapters set the stage for conducting effective literature circles in your classroom, regardless of the grade level. Beginning with understanding the theoretical underpinnings, it is important to articulate why literature discussions move learning and teaching forward. Through Vygotsky's (1978) notions of social learning and language as a primary tool for thinking and Rosenblatt's (1978, 1994) understandings of reader response, we come to recognize the valuable impact literature circles can have on students' constructions of meaning. Interpretations are shared in socially situated settings, and readers bring to the conversation their own backgrounds and experiences. The diversity of responses provides space for new interpretations to emerge.

Before starting a literature circle, four factors are important to consider: group composition, text selection, stance, and patterns of talk. Group composition and text selection play significant roles, particularly when the whole class is reading the same text. It is important to have students of varying abilities work together. Students learn many new ideas from peers. The literature selection should reflect high quality in literary and expository elements.

Interpretations are shared in socially situated settings, and readers bring to the conversation their own backgrounds and experiences.

Issues of stance and patterns of talk in the discussion also contribute to the foundation of successful literature discussions. Introduced was the continuum of efferent and aesthetic stances. Recall that efferent means to read to gain information while aesthetic stance is to read for the escapist, "lived through" feelings discussed by Rosenblatt (1994). The instructional stance you adopt for a reading event will influence the stance students adopt while engaged in a literature circle. Establishing response-centered discussions whereby students explore multiple discourse roles provides room for divergent and alternative interpretations to be heard. These divergent responses enhance the quality of the discussion.

With the foundation laid, strategies for literature circles with emerging and independent readers were shared. Before, during, and after reading strategies provide ways for you to begin your own discussions in your classroom. Conducting inquiry cycles and developing text sets add to effective literature circles.

Finally, alternative assessment strategies were addressed. Many ideas for reflecting on how your students interact and engage in literature circles were shared. Most significant are the opportunities for systematic observation. Stepping away from directing and controlling the discussion to observe how students facilitate their own discussions enables you to gain valuable information. Self-reporting evaluations and rubrics are opportunities for students to contribute to their own assessments.

The linear nature of the text suggests that each of these aspects happen independently of the others. The opposite is true. All of these come together through multiple ways to enable students to construct meaningful interpretations of text and to make such interpretations public. How you set up the discussion, the stance you adopt, and the types of discourse roles you allow students to assume will greatly impact the responses students share. Additionally, the questions asked and the amount of teacher presence contribute to or inhibit creative and mindful interpretations. Students involved in making some decisions about their discussion time, whether it is the group they are working with, the text to be read, or the follow-up activities, is another factor in the construction of meaningful literature circles.

Where does that leave us? There are new questions and new directions in the field of literacy development. We continue to think about how to further engage students who are initially viewed as reluctant readers in literature circles. Are there more useful strategies that bring them into the circle early? Consideration is needed in the area of emergent readers, as well. How successful are these discussions in helping students to construct their own understandings of text? Moreover, is there a balance between personal response and text response? Should students be able to rely only on one or the other to construct meaning?

Literature circles are viable and exciting aspects of language arts programs throughout the country.

These questions are but a few that continue to be important to the development of literacy in the elementary classrooms. Literature circles are viable and exciting aspects of language arts programs throughout the country. They manifest themselves in many different ways and for many different purposes. As we explore new avenues with literature discussions, I am delighted to have new colleagues with whom to discover uncharted territories.

References

Almasi, J. (1996). <u>A new view of discussion.</u> In L. Gambrell & J. Almasi (Eds.), <u>Lively discussions!: Fostering engaged reading.</u> (pp. 2–24). Newark, DE: International Reading Association.

Atwell, N. (1987). <u>In the middle.</u> Upper Montclair, NJ: Boynton/Cook.

Barrentine, S. (1996). Storytime plus dialogue equals interactive read alouds. In L. Gambrell & J. Almasi (Eds.), <u>Lively discussions!: Fostering engaged reading.</u> (pp. 52–62). Newark, DE: International Reading Association.

Bisesi, T. & Raphael, T. (1997). Assessment research in the book club program. In S. McMahon & T. E. Raphael, with V. Goatley & L. Pardo (Eds.), <u>The Book Club connection: Literacy learning and classroom talk.</u> (pp. 184–204). New York: Teachers College Press.

Britton, J. (1993). <u>Language and learning.</u> Portsmouth, NH: Heinemann.

Bruner, J. (1986). <u>Actual minds, possible worlds.</u> Cambridge, MA: Harvard University Press.

Calkins, L. (1994). <u>The art of teaching writing</u> (new edition). Portsmouth, NH: Heinemann.

Cazden, C. (1988). <u>Classroom discourse.</u> Portsmouth, NH: Heinemann.

Children's Book Council (1992). <u>Children's books: Awards and prizes.</u> New York: Children's Book Council.

Cox, C. & Many, J. E. (1989). Worlds of possibilities in literature, film, and life. <u>Language Arts,</u> 66, 287–294.

Cox, C. & Many, J. E. (1992). Stance towards a literary work: Applying the transactional theory to children's responses. <u>Reading Psychology,</u> 13, 37–72.

Cullinan, B. E. & Galda, L. (1994). <u>Literature and the child.</u> (3rd Edition). Fort Worth, TX: Harcourt Brace.

Dewey, J. (1916). <u>Democracy in education</u>. New York: Collier Macmillan.

Fish, S. (1980). <u>Is there a text in this class? The authority of interpretive communities.</u> Cambridge, MA: Harvard University Press.

Flint, A. S. (1997). Building sand castles and why Ralph and Keith are friends: The influences of stance, intertextuality, and interpretive authority on meaning construction. Unpublished doctoral dissertation, University of California, Berkeley, Berkeley, CA.

Gates, A. I. (1937). The necessary mental age for beginning reading. <u>Elementary School Journal,</u> 37, 497–508.

Graves, D. (1983). <u>Writing: Teachers and children at work.</u> Portsmouth, NH: Heinemann.

Gray, W. S. (1924). The importance of intelligent silent reading. <u>Elementary School Journal,</u> 24, 348–356.

Grisham, D. & Molinelli, P. (1995). <u>Professional's guide: Cooperative learning.</u> Westminster, CA: Teacher Created Materials.

Guthrie, J., Ng, M., McCann, A., Van Meter, P., & Alao, S. (1995). How do classroom characteristics influence intrinsic motivations for literacy? (Research Report). Athens, GA: Universities of Maryland and Georgia, National Reading Research Center.

Halliday, M. A. K. (1975). <u>Learning how to mean.</u> London: Arnold.

Heath, S. B. (1983). <u>Ways with words.</u> Cambridge: Cambridge University Press.

Hiebert, E. H. (1983). An examination of ability grouping for reading instruction. <u>Reading Research Quarterly,</u> 18, 231–255.

Hymes, D. (1972). Models of the interaction of language and social life. In J. J. Gumperz & D. Hymes (Eds.), <u>Directions in sociolinguistics: The ethnography of communication.</u> New York: Hold, Rinehart, and Winston.

Langer, J. (1995). <u>Envisioning literature.</u> New York: Teachers College Press.

Lapp, D., Flood, J., Ranck-Buhr, W., Van Dyke, J., & Spacek, S. (1997). "Do you really just want us to talk about this book?": A closer look at book clubs as an instructional tool. In J. Paratore & R. McCormack, (Eds.), <u>Peer talk in the classroom: Learning from research.</u> (pp. 6–23). Newark, DE: International Reading Association.

Many, J. (1989). Age level differences in children's use of an aesthetic stance when responding to literature. Unpublished doctoral dissertation, Louisiana State University, Baton Rouge, LA.

Matanzo, J. B. (1996). Discussion: Assessing what was said and what was done. In L. Gambrell & J. Almasi (Eds.), <u>Lively discussions!: Fostering engaged reading.</u> (pp. 250–264). Newark, DE: International Reading Association.

Mazzoni, S. & Gambrell, L. (1996). Text talk: Using discussion to promote comprehension of informational text. In L. Gambrell & J. Almasi (Eds.), <u>Lively discussions!: Fostering engaged reading.</u> (pp. 134–148). Newark, DE: International Reading Association.

McGee, L. (1995). Talking about books with young children. In N. Roser & M. Martinez (Eds.), <u>Book talk and beyond: Children and teachers respond to literature.</u> (pp. 105–115). Newark, DE: International Reading Association.

McMahon, S. (1997). Book clubs: Contexts for students to lead their own discussions. In S. McMahon & T. E. Raphael, with V. Goatley & L. Pardo (Eds.), The Book Club connection: Literacy learning and classroom talk. (pp. 89–106). New York: Teachers College Press.

Mehan, H. (1979). Learning lessons. Cambridge, MA: Harvard University Press.

Morrice, C. & Simmons, M. (1991). Beyond reading buddies: A whole language cross-aged program. Reading Teacher, 44(8), 572–579.

Pearson, P. D. (1985). Changing the face of reading comprehension. The Reading Teacher, 38(6), 724–738.

Raphael, T. E. & Boyd, F. (1997). When readers write: The Book Club writing component. In S. McMahon & T. E. Raphael, with V. Goatley & L. Pardo (Eds.), The Book Club connection: Literacy learning and classroom talk. (pp. 69–88). New York: Teachers College Press.

Raphael, T . E. Brock, C., & Wallace, S. (1997). Encouraging quality peer talk with diverse students in mainstream classrooms: Learning from and with teachers. In J. Paratore & R. McCormack, (Eds.), Peer talk in the classroom: Learning from research. (pp. 176–206). Newark, DE: International Reading Association.

Raphael, T. E. & Hiebert, E. H. (1996). Creating an integrated approach to literacy instruction. Fort Worth, TX: Harcourt Brace.

Raphael, T. E. & Goatley, V. (1997). Classrooms as communities: Features of community share. In S. McMahon & T. E. Raphael, with V. Goatley & L. Pardo (Eds.), The Book Club connection: Literacy learning and classroom talk. (pp. 26–46). New York: Teachers College Press.

Rhodes, L. & Shanklin, N. (1993). Windows into literacy: Assessing learners K–8. Portsmouth, NH: Heinemann.

Riordan-Karlsson, M. E. (1997). Negotiations, friendships, and chapter books: The influence of meaning authority, peer interaction, and student perceptions on reader motivation and meaning construction in a third grade classroom. Unpublished doctoral dissertation, University of California, Berkeley, Berkeley, CA.

Rosenblatt, L. M. (1978). The reader, the text, the poem: The transactional theory of the literary work. Carbondale, IL: Southern Illinois University Press.

Rosenblatt, L. M. (1994). The transactional theory of reading and writing. In R. B. Ruddell, M. R. Ruddell, & H. Singer (Eds.), Theoretical models and processes of reading (4th edition) (pp. 1057–1092). Newark, DE: International Reading Association.

Routman, R. (1994). Invitations: Changing as teachers and learners, K–12. Portsmouth, NH: Heinemann.

Ruddell, R. B. & Ruddell, M. R. (1995). Teaching children to read and write: Becoming an influential teacher. Needham Heights, MA: Allyn & Bacon.

Samway, K. D., Whang, G., Cade, C., Gamil, M., Lubandina, M., & Phommachanh, K. (1991). Reading the skeleton, the heart, and the brain of a book: Students' perspectives on literature study circles. The Reading Teacher, 45(3), 196–205.

Seely, A. E. (1994). Professional's guide: Portfolio assessment. Westminster, CA: Teacher Created Materials.

Short, K., Harste, J., & Burke, C. (1996). Creating classrooms for authors and inquirers (2nd edition). Portsmouth, NH: Heinemann.

Thorndike, E. L. (1921). The teacher's word bank. New York: New York Teachers College, Columbia University.

Valencia, S. (1990). A portfolio approach to classroom reading assessment: The whys, whats and hows. The Reading Teacher, 43, 338–340.

Vogt, M. E. (1996). Creating a response-centered curriculum with literature discussion groups. In L. Gambrell & J. Almasi (Eds.), Lively discussions!: Fostering engaged reading. (pp. 181–193). Newark, DE: International Reading Association.

Vygotsky, L. (1978). Mind in society. Cambridge, MA: Harvard University Press.

Wells, G. (1997). Learning to be literate. In S. McMahon & T. Raphael, with V. Goatley & L. Pardo (Eds.), The Book Club connection: Literacy learning and classroom talk. (pp. 107–118). New York: Teachers College Press.

Children's Literature

Adler, D. (1989). We remember the Holocaust. Henry, Holt, & Co.

Armstrong, R. (1996). Drew and the Bub Daddy showdown. HarperCollins.

Bemelmans, L. (1977). Madeline. Puffin Books.

Blume, J. (1971). Freckle juice. Four Winds Press.

Blume, J. (1972) Otherwise known as Sheila, the Great. Dell Publishing.

Cherry, L. (1990). The great kapok tree. Harcourt, Brace, & Jovanovich.

Cherry, L. (1991). A river ran wild. Harcourt, Brace, & Jovanovich.

Cleary, B. (1965). Mouse and the motorcycle. Avon Books.

Cohen, B. (1983). Molly's pilgrim. Lothrop, Lee, and Shepard.

Cohen, M. (1985). Starring first grade. Dell Publishing.

Creech, S. (1994). Walk two moons. HarperCollins.

DeCesare, A. (1996). <u>Anthony the perfect monster.</u> Random House.

Fleming, D. (1996). <u>Where once there was a wood.</u> Henry, Holt, & Co.

Grossman, B. (1996). <u>My little sister ate one hare.</u> Crown.

Heckman, P. (1996). <u>Waking upside down.</u> Atheneum.

Helmreich, W. (1993). <u>Against all odds: Holocaust survivors and the successful lives they made in America.</u> Simon and Schuster.

Henkes, K. (1996). <u>Chrysanthemum.</u> Mulberry Books.

Henkes, K. (1996). <u>Lilly's purple plastic purse.</u> Greenwillow.

Howe, J. (1987). <u>I wish I were a butterfly.</u> New York: Harcourt, Brace & Co.

Hudson, C. W. & Ford, B. (1990). <u>Bright eyes, brown skin.</u> Not Just Us Books (Sundance).

Hutchins, P. (1993). <u>My best friend.</u> Greenwillow.

Lorbiecki, M. (1996). <u>Just one flick of a finger.</u> Dial.

Lowry, L. (1989). <u>Number the stars.</u> Houghton Mifflin.

MacLachlan, P. (1987). <u>Sarah, plain and tall.</u> HarperCollins.

Matas, C. 1993). <u>Daniel's story.</u> Scholastic.

McCloskey, R. (1948) <u>Blueberries for Sal.</u> Viking Press.

Naylor, P. R. (1995) <u>Ice.</u> Atheneum.

Nikola-Lisa, W. (1994). <u>Bein' with you this way.</u> Lee & Low Books.

Novak, M. (1996). <u>Newt.</u> HarperCollins.

O'Dell, S. (1960). <u>Island of the blue dolphins.</u> Dell Publishing.

Pipe, J. (1996) <u>In the footsteps of the werewolf.</u> Copper Beach/Millbrook.

Rathman, P. (1995). <u>Officer Buckle and Gloria.</u> Putnam Publishing.

Rylant, C. (1985). <u>Every living thing.</u> Bradbury.

Simon, S. (1995). <u>Sharks.</u> Scholastic.

Spinelli, J. (1996). <u>Crash.</u> Knopf.

Stine, R. L. (1995). <u>Goosebumps: Night of terror tower.</u> Scholastic.

Volavkova, H. (1978). <u>I never saw another butterfly: Children's drawings and poems from Terezin concentration camp, 1942–1944.</u> Schochen Books.

Watson, M. (1995). <u>The butterfly seeds.</u> Tambourine.

White, E. B. (1952). <u>Charlotte's web.</u> HarperCollins Publishers.

Wood, A. (1996). <u>Bright and early Thursday evening: A tangled tale.</u> Harcourt Brace.

Yolen, J. (1988). <u>The devil's arithmetic.</u> Viking Press.

Teacher Created Materials Reference List

TCM 147 Activities for Any Literature Unit

TCM 210 Thematic Unit—Holocaust

TCM 353 Literature Activities for Reluctant Readers

TCM 504 Portfolios and Other Assessments

TCM 506 Middle School Assessment

TCM 780 Social Studies Assessment, Grades 5–6

TCM 2345 Literature Unit—<u>Freckle Juice, The Pain and the Great One,</u> and <u>The One in the Middle Is the Green Kangaroo</u>

Other References

Anne Frank Institute of Philadelphia
431 Chestnut St.
Lafayette Bldg., Suite 211
Philadelphia, PA 19106
215-625-0411

Holocaust Education and Memorial
Center of Toronto
4600 Bathurst St.
Willowdale, Ontario
M2R-3V2
Canada
416-635-2883

U.S. Holocaust Memorial Museum
100 Raoul Wallenberg Pl. SW
Washington, DC 20004-2150
202-488-0400